STAR CONSCIOUSNESS

DIRECT, MANAGE & TRANSFORM YOUR ENERGY

Dr. Greg Nielsen

Conscious Books
316 California Avenue, Ste. 210
Reno, Nevada 89509

Copyright © 2019, Greg Nielsen

All rights reserved. No part of this book may be reproduced or utilized in any form or by any means, electronic or mechanical, including photocopying, recording, videotaping, or by any information storage and retrieval system without permission in writing from the author. Inquiries should be addressed to the author c/o Conscious Books.

ISBN 978-0-9619917-5-3
10 9 8 7 6 5 4 3 2 1

Graphic Layout Design by Cyndee Bogard
Creative Consultant, Certified Marketing & Web Design
Website: http://www.cyndeebogard.com

Email: spiritualfrequenciesonline@gmail.com

Website: http://spiritualfrequencies.weebly.com/

Facebook: https://www.facebook.com/Spiritual-Frequencies-Online-Academy-1436072066656123/?ref=bookmarks

Instagram: spiritualfrequenciesacademy

Twitter: @FrequenciesDrG

YouTube Channel: https://www.youtube.com/channel/UCA8Rwm6Xl-4C8D131dqAkeIw?

Patreon: Where you can become a patron and financially support Spiritual Frequencies Online Academy for a modest monthly subscription. Patreon.com/spiritualfrequencies

Venmo: contribute directly to Conscious Books credit union account: @Greg-Nielsen-9

Other Books by Greg Nielsen:

RiverSpeak

MetaBusiness: Creating a New Global Culture

Tuning to the Spiritual Frequencies

Beyond Pendulum Power

Pendulum Power

Pyramid Power

Table of Contents

Prolog
Intro: Lost at Midnight in Bryce Canyon National Park　　8

Part 1: How to Expand Consciousness

Chapter 1: Sense-Based Consciousness　　22
Chapter 2: Self-Remembering　　24
Chapter 3: Self-Observation　　26
Chapter 4: Self-Reflection　　28
Chapter 5: Self-Knowledge　　30
Chapter 6: Self-Discovery　　32
Chapter 7: Self-Surrender　　34
Chapter 8: Star Consciousness　　36

Part 2: How to Live-Function as an Energy Being

Chapter 1: The Frequency-Energy World　　40
Chapter 2: Positive, Negative, Neutral Energies　　46
Chapter 3: Non-Identification　　51
Chapter 4: Rhythmic Alternation　　56
Chapter 5: Resonance, Reflection, Rapports　　60
Chapter 6: Automatic Energies　　64
Chapter 7: Relating Energies　　69
Chapter 8: Intuitive Energies　　72
Chapter 9: Creative Energies　　76
Chapter 10: Transformative Energies　　80
Chapter 11: A Fully Functioning Energy Being　　85
Chapter 12: Aligning with Star Consciousness　　90
Epilog
Appendix

"This work is beautiful when you see why it exists and what it means. It is about liberation. It is beautiful, as if locked for years in prison, you see a stranger entering who offers you a key. You have acquired prison-habits forgetting your origin, which is from the stars."

Maurice Nicoll, physician, psychiatrist, author of *Psychological Commentaries*

"I regard consciousness as fundamental. I regard matter as a derivative from consciousness. We cannot get behind consciousness. Everything we talk about, everything we regard as existing postulates consciousness."

Max Planck, Nobel Prize in Physics

"The only dominant theory we have of consciousness says that it is associated with complexity – with a system's ability to act upon its own state and determine its own fate."

Chirstof Koch, neuroscientist, Allen Institute for Brain Science.

"If you want to awaken all of humanity then awaken all of yourself. If you want to eliminate the suffering in the world, then eliminate all that is dark and negative in yourself. Truly, the greatest gift you have to give is that of your own self-transformation."

Lao Tzu

"We come from the stars, literally. You may have heard we are stardust, and you thought it was something poetic, something that was kind of a nice analogy, but your body literally had to be forged inside a star that died. And the amazing thing is that, if you ever wanted a connection to a larger universe, you already have it. You don't need to go looking for it. It's

right here inside you. It's not just a single star either. The Sun has been around the Galaxy about 20 times since our star formed. And that means that we swept up material from stars clear across the galaxy, stars that are hundreds of thousands of light-years away when they died, we've been through their clouds, their material is in us today."

Michelle Thaller, astrophysicist, NASA

"The cosmos is within us. We are made of star stuff. We are a way for the cosmos to know itself."

Carl Sagan author of *Cosmos*

"Then I saw that on the shaft there hung a human figure that held within itself all the loneliness of the world and of the spaces. Alone, and hoping for nothing, he hung and gazed down into the void. For long the one gazed, drawing all solitude unto itself. Then deep in the fathomless dark was born an infinitesimal spark. Slowly, it rose from the bottomless depth, and as it rose it grew until it became a star. And the star hung in space just opposite the figure, and the White Light streamed upon the lonely one."

From *The Inner Word of Man*, Frances Wickes

Prolog

I watched The Farthest: Voyager in Space (PBS) on Netflix. This documentary chronicles NASA's 1977 launch of twin space probes to capture images of remote solar system planets. After billions of miles Voyager passed Jupiter, Saturn, Neptune and Uranus. Voyager continued passed the outer planets eventually reaching the edge of the solar system in 2012. The Sun's magnetic field bubble membrane was penetrated and Voyager entered Interstellar Space.

I fell asleep at the conclusion of the documentary. I dreamed I was in Interstellar Space observing the remote light years path of Voyager. In that vast distance in Interstellar Space I saw a streak of white light. I knew it was intelligent consciousness also traveling through Interstellar Space. I woke up energized and keenly conscious.

Introduction:

Lost at Midnight in Bryce Canyon National Park

It was year nine of the Dane & Daddypants National Park Tour. Dane is my son, amigo, and Senor Dane. I'm Daddypants. Don't ask me why I'm called Daddypants. His friends call me Daddypants too. In nine years we visited twelve National Parks. Dane's favorite was Crater Lake National Park and mine was Grand Teton National Park.

In the summer of 2018 we visited Bryce Canyon National Park. By synchronicity and serendipity, we arrived at Bryce Canyon on the weekend of the 18th Annual Bryce Canyon Astronomy Festival. We went to Dr. Michelle Thaller's talk *We Are Dead Stars*. You can Google the title and watch her talk on YouTube or TED. Here's the part that really gave us a shot of consciousness Scotch.

> *"We come from the stars, literally. You may have heard we are star stuff, and you thought it was something poetic, something that was kind of a nice analogy, but your body literally had to be forged inside a star that died. And the amazing thing is that, if you ever need to go looking for it, it's right here inside you…You are the galaxy…the iron that makes your blood red was created in a Super Nova on the other side of the Milky Way Galaxy!*

After Dr. Thaller's talk, Dane and I were spaced, our consciousnesses wandered outside the three-dimensional world we were used to. Driving back to Bryce Canyon Lodge at midnight, we seemed to float through space-time with the tires not really touching the highway. In fact, we were lost. We saw no signs, no hotel lights, no familiar landmarks.

When you're lost you're disoriented and apprehensive. The imagination runs wild with scenario speculations. Fifty years before my dad and I got lost in the Swiss Alps at noon. I wrote about how it felt. "Worry, anxiety, fear and frustration repeatedly shook our nerves. Our ankles and arches ached. Salty sweat trickled and ran into our eyes. Our minds raced with: What are we going to do? How are we going to get back? Why did we come this way?

Dane and I figured we missed the turn leading back to the lodge. We drove through the black void night on a windy road, a spiral galaxy highway. There were no lights from buildings or headlights from cars; we were in an earthly black hole. We were panicky, but we didn't panic. We decided the worst-case scenario was pulling off the road and sleeping in the car until daybreak.

Eventually, we turned around and drove slowly, about ten miles per hour, back toward the lodge turn off. Dr. Thaller's talk launched us into a kind of altered reality where we had no compass, no sense of direction. We were star dust blowing in the cosmic wind. We made it back to Bryce Canyon Lodge with a mind-altering experience. Fifty years earlier, my dad and I made it back to Leysin, Switzerland because we happened to come across girl scouts hiking on the trail.

Star Consciousness - literally, we are star consciousness. Generally, there are two schools of thought about consciousness. Astronomer Dr. Greg Matloff expresses it as follows:
1. Consciousness is an emergent property of brain function: it arises in brains when neural networks become sufficiently complex.
2. Consciousness permeates the universe and all matter and is, to a certain extent, conscious.

Here we combine both and say consciousness is axiomatic. If you deny or doubt consciousness, with what power to you deny or doubt? It's self-evident and needs no proof?

Dr. Matloff proposes that "consciousness emerges in molecules through an interaction with a universal proto-consciousness-field that is congruent or identical with vacuum fluctuations. Stars cool enough to possess upper layers with stable molecules that are more conscious than hotter stars and move differently to participate in galactic self-organization."

The next afternoon Dane and I opened a bottle of Scotch. It's a ritual we celebrate on the Dane and Daddypants National Park Tour. It's our communion. Scotch and ice rather than unleavened bread and wine. Our talking crosses the line into verbal riffing. That afternoon I wandered into memories, dreams and reflections about my past focusing on how I climbed onto the Pegasus of consciousness. He took notes. When I finished the short history of my galactic earth voyage, he said, "You need to write about it in your new book, Star Consciousness."

Here is what I said as best I can recall. I was born in Minot, North Dakota on Mother's Day, the second Sunday in May. According to my mother my birth was announced on radio. My parents named me Gregory Alan Nielsen. Gregory after the movie star Gregory Peck, my mother's favorite actor and Alan after Alan Ladd, also a famous actor. He was my father's favorite actor.

Rather than focus mostly on ego Greg, both a foe and a friend, I'm going to highlight memories, dreams and reflections similar to the autobiography of the Swiss psychologist, Carl Jung. As a teenager I read his *Memories, Dreams and Reflections*. Have you ever read a book that changed your life? Reading his autobiography inspired me to explore the inner world, the spiritual path, *The Hero with a Thousand Faces* [title of a book my Joseph Campbell].

By the time I was in Kindergarten I attended choir school on Saturday mornings. I sang in the children's choir at my local church. I especially loved singing at Easter time. I volunteered to sing at all five services beginning with the sunrise service often held outside. The energy felt rejuvenating and the celebration of the rebirth of Jesus held me with a fascinating numinosity.

At sixteen I enrolled in Saturday morning catechism classes at church. By this time, we had moved to Wayzata, Minnesota and joined another church. I was intensely interested in what the religion I was born into believed. I attended every class and took notes during the minister's Sunday sermon. I meticulously completed all the required training and homework. I began to think critically about the Christian beliefs. I wondered, asked questions, challenged and began thinking for myself rather than swallowing the religion whole and mechanically believing.

I was one of two students selected from our catechism class who did outstanding work. We were given a trip to the Black Hills in South Dakota in order to see the Passion Play performance in nearby Spearfish, South Dakota. Our lead pastor had a pilot's license and flew us from Minneapolis, Minnesota to Rapid City, South Dakota in a small passenger plane. The flight was spectacular and exciting with a pinch of trepidation.

The Passion Play was gripping. It was a dramatic re-enactment of the death of Jesus on the cross at Calgary to Jesus's resurrection three days later from a tomb. This experience really got me thinking. Did this really happen? Was it a made-up story that I was simply to believe without question? Or was it symbolical or metaphorical about some spiritual process or evolution? I don't know about you but once I started asking a lot of questions I journeyed down an unlit path of doubt and disbelief that led me to search and research. I read. I challenged. At times, I bordered on atheism.

The next seven years turned out to be the most turbulent, disruptive and transformative years of my life. Dissatisfaction, disappointment, depression, death and disease had me passing through the entrance to the underworld and into the dark night of the soul.

When I turned seventeen I was itching to be independent and do something adventurous. I decided to take a road trip to the Grand Teton mountains in Wyoming and learn how to mountain climb. I approached my parents asking if I could use one of the family cars in order to journey to the Tetons with two friends. They were not too keen on the idea, especially my mother.

Regardless, I had this desire to answer the call to adventure in order to explore and be on my own. I began to secretly plot how I was going to take one of the family cars and drive to the Rocky Mountains of Colorado. I decided to run away and start a life on my own. I didn't consider the consequences. How would I support myself? Where would I live? I had no job or contacts in Colorado.

One summer night between my junior and senior years of high school, I packed a bag, gathered some food from the kitchen and stuffed my wallet with my savings. I pushed the car out of the garage and down the driveway in order not to make any sounds. I drove off into the black night and headed west to Colorado. I drove all night. It was exhilarating. I was totally on my own. By daybreak, I was exhausted. I was near the Nebraska-Colorado border. I pulled off the highway and fell into a deep sleep.

When I awoke, I started to come to my senses, realizing it wasn't such a good idea to run away from home. I turned around and headed home to Wayzata, Minnesota. Needless to say, my parents were not happy and were worried for my safety. They had reported me missing to the police.

The look on their faces when I returned was a mixture of relief and anger. I realized I had put an unsettling scare into them. My dad sat down with me in the living room to talk about what happened. I told him I needed to do something independent by taking a trip to the Grand Tetons with friends. He listened giving me the nod to go ahead. In August, I traveled with two friends to Wyoming where I took climbing lessons with the world-renowned climber Glen Exum. I learned enough to climb the Grand Teton.

The following year, after graduating from high school, I returned to the Tetons in early August. This time I traveled alone. It was a week before I was to report to Colorado College in Colorado Springs for my freshman year. I didn't have a word for it then but essentially, I was going on a vision quest or a walkabout. I sought an experience that provided a clue to what life path I needed to follow.

I did have three experiences that spoke to me. As I neared the Wyoming Wind River mountain range on a full moon night, thousands of jack rabbits stampeded across the highway. It was eerie. I must have run over at least a hundred rabbits. Apparently, they were drawn to the headlights. That was the logical reason. But part of me wondered what the lesson was, the metaphorical reason. I slowed down to about 20 miles per hour and turned off my headlights. There was a full moon, so I could easily see the highway. I killed fewer rabbits.

When the stampede was over, I turned the headlights back on and drove until about 2 a.m. I pulled off the highway in order to sleep. As I laid back on the front seat, I noticed a bright light on a distant mountain top. Was it a cabin? Was it a forest ranger tower? I searched for a logical, objective reason.

One by one I eliminated each possible reason. Finally, I was left with an illogical reason. Was it a UFO hovering over the mountain top? Carl Jung in his autobiography *Memories, Dreams and Reflections* addressed the UFO phenomenon saying it was a kind of dream symbol of person's integrated self. I continued gazing at the mysterious bright light. Thoroughly exhausted, I fell asleep. A few hours later I woke up and drove the last hour to Grand Teton National Park in Jackson Hole, Wyoming. I pitched my tent at the climber's camp at Jennie Lake.

The third thing that happened on my vision quest happened on a hike by myself to Lake Solitude about ten miles into the high Teton back country. Lake Solitude is serene and ultra-Zen. After eating lunch, I chose not to walk back the way I came. Instead, I continued up to the top of the pass to hike down on the other side of the mountain. Reaching the top of the pass, I walked around a bend in the trail. I was stunned to see a man about 19 or 20 years old dressed in a military uniform sitting on a rock at the top of the pass.

I asked him what he was doing there. He said he had jumped off a train passing through Jackson Hole. The Vietnam War was raging, and I was apprehensive of being drafted into the military. I had recently registered for the draft and received an exemption for being enrolled in college.

The young man had a name above his uniform right

pocket. It read in bold, capital letters: LOVE. It struck me as odd, as did the jack rabbit stampede and the possible UFO. He was apparently deployed to Vietnam and his last name was LOVE. My mind was spiraling with random thoughts.

The Beatle's song, *All You Need Is Love*, played in my mind. I had seen Vietnam War protests on television chanting "make love, not war." LOVE and I decided to hike back to Jennie Lake, a good three-hour hike. I know we talked between long silences. I can't recall exactly what we discussed. Maybe we talked about how he felt about going to war. I learned that he was AWOL (Absent Without Leave). I thought about what would happen to him when he returned to duty. I know he told me his first name, but I can't remember now.

Reaching the north end of Jennie Lake, we decided to split up. He would take the west trail and I would take the east trail and see who made it back to camp first. I cheated. I was crazy competitive in those days. I hitched a ride on the back of a camper. There's no doubt I arrived first. I waited for LOVE at the end of the west trail. He never showed. There's no way he could have hiked back before me.

I asked around the campground to see if they had seen a man dressed in an Army uniform. He would have stood out like a sore thumb. No one had seen him. Finally, I went to the park ranger station and asked about the train that ran through Jackson Hole. The ranger told me there was no train that ran through Jackson Hole. I was baffled. Was LOVE real? Was our encounter in some altered reality?

Several years later I read about the shaman ally in Carlos Castaneda's book *Don Juan the Yaqui Indian*. It hit me. I had met with an ally. He had something to teach me. I now was consciously following a spiritual path. LOVE in an Army uniform had manifested giving me some direction, insight and wisdom about my path.

A few days later I left the Tetons somewhat mystified. I drove to Colorado Springs for the start of football training camp at Colorado College. My freshman year began two weeks later.

Before the third game of the season I got knocked out in practice. It was my third concussion. My first concussion was at nine when I fell while ice skating. The second occurred in a football game my senior year in high school.

My college coach, learning of the previous concussions, sent me to the team doctor. He refused to clear me to play. He told me my season was over. It was too dangerous. Another concussion and it could result in brain damage. I was angry at the doctor. He was way ahead of his time. I'm deeply thankful to him now.

My whole world was turned upside down. Sports had been the cornerstone of my life since I was in Little League baseball at nine. Suddenly, I had lots of free time. I began to write poetry and I discovered The Flick, a theater in Colorado Springs featuring foreign films from around the world.

I thought more and more about the Vietnam War. I researched. Listened to experts. I joined the SDS, Students for a Democratic Society. I traveled to a peace march in San Francisco. I seriously began to consider becoming a conscientious objector and even leaving America seeking asylum in Canada or Sweden. In good conscience I could not support the war based on the United States government's lies.

The year at Colorado College expanded my horizons to the point that I could no longer stay. It was too narrow-minded, and star spangled American. I really did not fit in. I transferred to the University of Minnesota (U of M) in Minneapolis where my interests in poetry, film and protesting the war could be expressed more openly. I discovered my major: Humanities. Decades later I began teaching Humanities at the University of Nevada after earning a doctorate in education.

During my first semester at the U of M, I visited home one weekend. I received a life changing shock. What English psychologist, Dr. Maurice Nicoll, called a conscious shock. It was nuclear. I walked into the bedroom my brother Mike and I shared and found him dead on the bed, a bullet through his heart. Apparently, he either had a gun accident or committed suicide.

His untimely death shattered my world. I was cast into a thousand pieces. I descended into the underworld of why. Why did he die? What happens at death? Is there an afterlife? Why are we here? Why was I here?

Over the next two years I was consumed by grief. Depression, emotional agony and psychological numbness plagued me. At times, I acted like an automaton just going through the motions of living. I did read a lot. I kept my eyes and ears open for hints and clues to answering the whys.

The following summer break from the U of M I backpacked around Europe for three months. It was another vision quest. Getting away often opens perception and attracts experiences and people that infuse meaning and purpose into your life. For two weeks my dad came to Europe. We traveled together.

We stayed in a youth hostel in Leysin, Switzerland. On a day hike we got lost in the Swiss Alps. Getting lost together and surviving created an emotional bond and bridged the generation gap between The Greatest Generation and the Baby Boomer Generation.

Still, the most meaningful experience of the Europe vision quest was visiting the Greek Islands. I knew nothing about reincarnation or past lives. I felt a profound sense of peace. I was home; I felt strangely that I had lived on the Greek Islands in a previous life or lives.

At the end of my vision quest I returned to the U of M with the decision to become a screenwriter and a film director. I enrolled in two film classes, film history and film making. I wrote and directed three short student films, *Used Car*, *The Empty School House* and *Vietnam Bombs*, an animated short. I believed I found my calling.

The following spring break I attended the New York Film Festival in Manhattan. I loved New York City especially Greenwich Village and Washington Square Park. Every day was a happening filled with innovative films, music, art, antiwar protestors, and spiritual seekers. I truly discovered happiness when I was creative and following my life path and purpose.

The day after I returned to the U of M I woke up feeling extremely drained. At first, I thought I was tired from the flight back from NYC. I got ready and struggled to walk to my first class. I realized that there was something very physically wrong. I was so weak it took all I had to make it to campus. Instead of walking to my class I walked to the University of Minnesota Hospital.

I entered the hospital. The check in nurse immediately recognized I was in desperate straits. I barely maintained consciousness. She checked me in. For three agonizing weeks the doctors did not know what I had. I was in limbo. I didn't know if I was going to live or die. Finally, they diagnosed me with a life-threatening blood cancer, aplastic anemia. My immune system was compromised with a low white blood cell count. The iron rich red blood cells were not healthy either, the source of my weak feeling.

I had a dream. In the dream I had a choice to live or die. It was clearly an open choice. Either way it would be okay. I wrestled with the decision. I chose to live. With that choice I decided to dedicate myself to a spiritual path that would seek out meaningful answers to the whys. From that day on I fully embraced my life and did whatever it took to make each day fulfilling, meaningful and creative.

While in the hospital, I received blood transfusions. They literally kept me alive. I'm thankful to those who donated blood so I could live. I read, wrote poetry, continued my spring classes with tutors, played the guitar and maintained a positive attitude. After a couple of months I was able to go home in between blood transfusions.

By fall, I was recovering to the point that I didn't need any more transfusions. The medication seemed to stimulate blood regeneration. Still, the doctors warned me that there was a fifty-fifty chance of a relapse within five years.

Coming face to face with death, I decided to do what I was called to do. Rather than go back and finish college, I chose to pursue my dreams in film by moving to Southern California and write screenplays. I'm thankful to my parents for supporting that radical decision. It is a dreamer's dream, one that often leads to a broken dream. Thirty plus years later Dane had a dream to become a working actor in Los Angeles. I supported that dream partly out of gratitude to my parents for supporting mine. I ended up living in Laguna Beach.

My next-door neighbor, who recently was released from prison for selling weed, turned me on to a spiritual bookstore, Mystic Arts World, founded by Timothy Leary and John Griggs. The acid known as Orange Sunshine was dispensed from the store. I visited the store daily purchasing books on Eastern religions, meditation, healing and cosmic consciousness. I read voraciously. I practiced meditation and became more mindful of being in the moment, a state of wordless awareness.

One day in serendipity I decided to call my friend Molly from Minnesota. She had moved to New York City to live with her sister Julie. As I walked along the beach I saw a payphone and called. Molly and I chatted catching up on the last couple of months. She told me I needed to talk with her sister's boyfriend and guru who studied Carl Jung and others. She knew I loved Jung's autobiography, *Memories, Dreams and Reflections*.

Francois got on the phone. He gave me an introduction to what he was learning and teaching. His words reinforced and resonated with all the reading I had done while in Laguna Beach. I seized the moment. I compellingly asked, "This is going to sound crazy, but I'd like to come to New York and study with you." There was silence; it seemed like it lasted five minutes. It was probably only one minute but it seemed like a long time. He broke the silence by saying yes. That yes turned out to be the most important sound in my life up to that point. I told him I'd be there in a few days.

I arrive in New York at the end of December. Again, I'm eternally grateful to my parents for supporting my dreamer's quest. When I met Francois, I knew I had made a monumentally life changing decision. He was a student of Joseph Campbell, who, I found out, was the foremost scholar of comparative religions.

For the next two years I devoted myself to studying the world literature on spiritual paths. It was the most exhilarating time in my life. I even met Joseph Campbell at the Cooper Union lecture hall at New York University. Just as my spiritual consciousness grew wings unexpectedly Francois died of a heart attack at thirty-eight.

I was devastated but not as much as when my brother Mike died. Fortunately, Francois had introduced us to Isidore Friedman, another teacher on the spiritual path. For the next decade I studied Organics: The Law of the Breathing Spiral with Izzy, as he was affectionally called. My training transitioned from intellectual knowing to functional knowing, from thought and talk to walking the walk, from being an identifier with things to learning to direct, manage and transform my energies – Star Consciousness.

Part 1: How to Expand Consciousness

Chapter 1: Sense-Based Consciousness

In order to align and resonate with star consciousness, which is the skill and wisdom to direct, manage and transform life energy, there are practical and functional steps that can be taken. First, you need to notice and acknowledge sensory awareness. That's obvious, right? But, do you actively notice when you see, hear, taste, touch and smell?

By paying acute attention to sensory awareness you acknowledge and enhance sense-based consciousness. Why bother? If you feel an inner-urge to know more, to self-discover, to align with life purpose, to experience a state of energetic equilibrium, then taking this first step will open the gate to star consciousness.

Once you cross this threshold, you will feel a call to adventure. Being mechanically content with automaton unconsciousness will not suffice. The adventure leads to discovering what it means to be fully human. Having human form doesn't necessarily mean you are a functioning human being. To be fully human requires non-identification with copying animals in nervous responses. This non-identification is an act of consciousness.

As potential humans we have the opportunity and choice to be more conscious. The alternative is unconsciousness, the automatic belief and acceptance that unenhanced sensory awareness is all that's required. Choosing unconsciousness is the refusal of the call to adventure that leads to star consciousness. An unconscious fog blankets the everyday world of work, entertainment, religion and politics. Blind belief, lack of awareness, fact denying, and self-destructive habits are the order of the day.

I invite you to begin your quest by committing just one day to what Leonardo Da Vinci labeled sensazione, the continual refinement of the senses. Enliven and enhance your sensory awareness from awakening to falling asleep for one whole day. What do you notice? Keep a journal. Write down your enhanced listening, touching, tasting, smelling and seeing. Discover what

Da Vinci discovered. He wrote, for example, about the sense of sight: "He who loses his sight loses, his view of the universe, and is like one interred alive [unconsciousness] who can still move about and breath in his grave." If you live to eighty-five, that's more than 30,000 days. Commit to just one day. Practice enhanced sensory awareness from the second you awake to the second you fall asleep.

Chapter 1 Summary:

1. In order to align and resonate with star consciousness, which is the skill and wisdom to direct, manage and transform life energy, there are practical and functional steps that can be taken.
2. If you feel an inner-urge to know more, to self-discover, to manifest your life purpose, to experience a state of energetic equilibrium, then taking this first step will open the gate to star consciousness.
3. Choosing unconsciousness is the refusal of the call to adventure that leads to star consciousness.
4. Enliven and enhance your sensory awareness from awakening to falling asleep for one whole day.

Chapter 2: Self-Remembering

Choosing to be conscious is self-remembering. When I was first introduced to self-remembering by a mentor and the book by Harry Benjamin, *Basic Self-Knowledge: An Introduction to Esoteric Psychology*, I went ahead and gave it a try. It seemed simple enough.

I said to myself, "I am completely aware in the here-now." Sometimes I'd even say it out loud. "I am completely aware in the here-now." In a flicker of a second the here-now consciousness accelerated my energy. Next, I noticed automatic thinking, the incessant mental chatter. Arrogantly, I thought, "okay, I got that. I know what self-remembering is."

In another flicker of second I sank back into a quagmire of unconscious, un-remembering. I didn't realize that self-remembering required sustained effort over an extended time. Self-remembering needed to be continuous. It sounded simple. The hard part was remembering to self-remember.

I was amazed how often I'd forget. The everyday "I" personality, the self-centered ego consciousness, obsessively identifies with its actions, hopes, dreams, fears, likes, dislikes, wishes, thoughts, desires, etc. Effectively, this excludes the revitalizing experience of self-remembering. It turns out when we let go of our self-centeredness we open up to a vast world of star consciousness.

Harry Benjamin writes – "Therefore, the act of self-remembering has been especially designed to break the complete sway of personality, and to make us aware – if only for brief flashes of time – of the existence of something far greater and deeper in us." In order to go from brief flashes of time to living more and more in the here-now and even, potentially, permanently, you will need to practice self-remembering day in and day out.

Realize the false personality will find every distraction under the sun to maintain its petty selfish ways. Persistent self-remembering transforms your consciousness. It opens a vast world of vibrations, frequencies, and energies characterized by peace of mind, emotional calm, focused relaxation, compassion and wisdom. "I am completely aware in the here-now."

Chapter 2 Summary:

1. Self-remembering requires sustained effort over an extended time. Self-remembering needs to be continuous.
2. It turns out when we let go of our self-centeredness we open up to a vast world of star consciousness.
3. Realize the false personality will find every distraction under the sun to maintain its petty selfish ways.
4. Self-remembering opens a vast world of vibrations, frequencies and energies characterized by peace of mind, emotional calm, focused relaxation, compassion and wisdom.

Chapter 3: Self-Observation

What is self-observation and why is it necessary in order to expand consciousness? As you go about your day to day life, you are doing, thinking, feeling, relating, speaking, emoting, desiring, and reacting. Generally, most everyone is vaguely aware of these life experiences. This, however, is not true self-observation. It's more of a superficial distorted, biased recording of experience.

Self-observation, as referred to here, goes deeper by accurately noticing how we function and behave both positive and negative. Sincerely committing yourself to self-observation will, at first, more than likely increase the ego's tendency to avoid seeing and openly acknowledging the negative and self-destructive reactions in favor of the often false-to-fact positive thoughts, feelings and actions.

This half-hearted self-observation leads to ego inflation, self-aggrandizement and a sense of superiority. When you notice negative thoughts, feelings and actions without sugarcoating them and without excuses, alibis and justifying you are expanding your consciousness. When you clearly notice making excuses, fabricating alibis and manufacturing justification without putting yourself down, harshly judging yourself, feeling excessive guilt and/or wallowing in self-pity, you are practicing true self-observation.

Self-indulging in excessive negative self-observation can be as unproductive to expanding consciousness as self-praise, ego pride and feelings of superiority for remarkable "successes". Instead, strive for an accurate, relatively balanced assessment that more and more sees without association, without overly positive or overly negative judgments.

This is true self-observation. It notices how you actually function, not how you think, feel or believe you function. In other words, you call a spade a spade. You use what can be called bare attention. You simply record the full spectrum of your functions. This skill leads inevitably and inexorably to a leap in your range of awareness, aligning and resonating you more and more with star consciousness.

Chapter 3 Summary:

1. Self-observation, as referred to here, goes deeper by accurately noticing how we function and behave both positive and negative.
2. When you notice negative thoughts, feelings and actions without sugarcoating them and without excuses, alibis and justifying you are expanding your consciousness.
3. The self-observation skill leads inevitably and inexorably to a leap in your range of awareness, aligning and resonating you more and more with star consciousness.

Chapter 4: Self-Reflection

Self-reflection expands consciousness even further. It goes beyond noticing without opinion, bias and/or justification. Self-reflection asks the question: Is this a behavior that I want to improve, eliminate and transform?

The act of self-reflection acknowledges change for the better. If you are identifying unconsciously and excessively with fear, anger, hate, self-centeredness, etc. then star consciousness, which is the skill and wisdom to direct, manage and transform your life energy, will have a diminished influence on your life.

In order to create change for the better, which raises the vibrations in your auric-field, you must practice non-identification. When you are acutely aware of an action, a behavior, an emotion, a way of speaking, etc. you want to improve or eliminate, you need to practice non-identification. Whatever you identify with, whether a thought, feeling, desire, belief or action you are providing the energy. When you detach from a belief you decide it is not in your best interest, you are non-identifying and thus reducing the energy required to continue the belief.

Let's say, for example, you believe that if you were wealthy you would be happy. As you make more and more money you, through self-observation and self-reflection, realize you are not happier. In fact, you may discover that you are less happy. Happiness can be defined as a state of physical repose, emotional calm and peace of mind.

These three skills cannot be purchased. They require effort, the conscious directing, managing and transforming of your life energy. If you are tense, you need to learn to relax and let go, a form of non-identification. If you are often in emotional turmoil, you need to be less automatically reactive, another form of non-identification. If you are obsessively thinking, you have little or no peace of mind.

You cannot buy peace of mind, emotional calm and physical repose at Walmart or Amazon.com. Money cannot buy happiness. Through self-reflection you can, over time, let go of a false belief and learn to manifest more happiness by changing your behavior. This leads to a greater resonance with star consciousness.

Chapter 4 Summary:

1. Self-reflection asks the question: Is this a behavior that I want to improve, eliminate or transform?
2. In order to create change for the better, which raises the vibrations in your auric-field, you must practice non-identification.
3. Happiness can be defined as a state of physical repose, emotional calm and peace of mind.
4. These three skills cannot be purchased. They require effort, the conscious directing, managing and transforming your life energy.
5. Through self-reflection you can, over time, let go of a false belief and learn to manifest more happiness by changing your behavior. This leads to a greater resonance with star consciousness.

Chapter 5: Self-Knowledge

Self-remembering, self-observation and self-reflection leads to self-knowledge. Why is self-knowledge essential to star consciousness? When you become aware of how you function – think, act, feel, desire, etc. – you can potentially control and even master your forces and energies.

Self-knowledge and self-mastery increases power. Power can be harnessed for good or ill. Self-knowledge demands flexible yet stringent control of your thoughts, feelings, desires and actions; the wise use of energy.

To date, science has mostly studied, learned and harnessed the forces of nature. The control of water, air, fire, electricity and sub-atomic particles has produced a tsunami of innovation and technology. In order to meet the ethical challenges that biotechnology, nuclear power, food production, artificial intelligence and climate change pose, scientific investigations must turn inward. This will require that more and more individuals heed the call to scientifically study themselves.

Traditionally, science often labels those who cultivate psycho-logical self-knowledge as "subjective" and "metaphysical" implying they are not scientific. After all, science is "objective" and is based on verifiable evidence. Neuroscience, among other scientific disciplines, is bridging the gap between "objective" science and "subjective" science opening the way to the scientific method being applied to psycho-logical and psycho-spiritual frequencies.

Self-knowledge necessitates persistence and a willingness to precisely uncover layers of previously unconscious behaviors observed on psycho-logical levels. This will, in most cases, mean seeing the tendencies toward self-censorship. Being honest and truthful with oneself recognizes the tendency to alter the facts, change the narrative to preserve the ego's "good" face.

Practicing and gathering self-knowledge will challenge you to go beyond ego aggrandizement and accept the fact that you are not all you believed you were cracked up to be. This emotional fortitude increases your emotional I.Q. and presents choices that either build character toward star consciousness or inflate the illusion, delusion and false power of ego centered selfishness.

Chapter 5 Summary:

1. When you become aware of how you function, think, act, feel, desire, etc., you can potentially control and even master your forces and energies.
2. In order to meet the ethical challenges that biotechnology, nuclear power, food production, artificial intelligence and climate change pose, scientific investigations must turn inward.
3. Practicing and gathering self-knowledge will challenge you to go beyond ego aggrandizement and accept the fact that you are not all you believed you were cracked up to be.

Chapter 6: Self Discovery

Self-knowledge inevitably opens up to a multitude of self-discoveries. We think/believe we know ourselves. For instance, you know you like ice cream. You know you don't like chocolate ice cream. You, generally, like ice cream only in the summer; you don't like it in the winter. This kind of self-knowing is superficial and applies to the everyday personality.

Self-knowledge that opens up to self-discoveries is deeper and less obvious. You discover habits, and behavior patterns that you were mostly or even completely unconscious of or thought was "normal." Why bother? Who really cares? What's the big deal? Star consciousness entails being conscious as much as possible. Whatever you're unconscious of controls you; whatever you're conscious of you begin to and eventually control. You cannot be out of control and align with star consciousness.

Here's a self-discovery I've come across in the last couple of years that I've become more conscious of – self-cursing. Previously, I didn't give it much thought. It's no big deal. Everybody does it. I was certainly aware of self-cursing in a superficial way when I forgot, misplaced, spilled, broke, or dropped something. I would self-curse. I might say to myself, 'damn, what an idiot.'

The self-discovery hit me one day. 'Why curse myself?' Putting myself down has a vibrational effect on my psyche/subconscious. I am giving myself a negative suggestion that attracts damning events or circumstances. One of my mentors gave me a functional tool for handling self-cursing along with a spectrum of other emotionally charged thoughts – register but don't react.

Gradually, I noticed the self-cursing had less of a negative, emotional charge loaded on it. In fact, there have been a few times where I just noticed; I forgot something and did not say out loud or to myself 'damn.' Okay, I forgot. Now retrieve what I forgot and go about my daily business. I realize it's not so bad. Besides, I fortunately remembered I forgot.

This self-discovery has led to giving myself more

patience, understanding, forgiveness and compassion. I've even chuckled to myself after a lapse of in the moment awareness after knocking over a cup of water. The spill shape on the floor revealed a beautiful pattern. I took a photo. Eventually, I had a several spill photos. I showed friends. They sent me their spill photos. I displayed the spill photos at an art show. The self-cursing habit transformed into an artistic experience.

Chapter 6 Summary:

1. Self-knowledge that opens up to self-discoveries is deeper and less obvious.
2. One of my mentors gave me a functional tool for handling emotionally charged thoughts – register but don't react.
3. Self-discovery will lead to giving yourself more patience, understanding, forgiveness and compassion.

Chapter 7: Self-Surrender

As you expand consciousness and increase self-knowledge, you naturally become more consciousness of the thoughts, feelings, desires and actions of others. The identification with you as a self-centered ego personality lessens. You see the benefits of surrendering your one-valued orientation.

Vitvan, the founder of The School of the Natural Order, provided star consciousness seeking students with the following meditation that involves self-surrender. Part 2 of this small book focuses on how to direct, manage and transform your energy. It takes energy to think, feel, desire and act. To practice this meditation, you need self-observation. Self-observe; notice where your energy is focused. Let go, surrender your identification with that energy as you. Vitvan writes: "The whole point [of this meditation] hinges on the surrender, giving up, offering in genuineness, in sincerity – almost in desperation – offering it all."

The more your self-knowledge evolves the more you will notice how intensely identified you are with your likes, dislikes, hopes, fears and desires. The first law of human energy is energy follows attention. When you let go of an obsessive fear, for instance, you are no longer feeding that fear energy. As you surrender fear, offer the energy to star consciousness.

Vitvan suggests you surrender by focusing "your thought at the crown of your head." Energy follows attention so the energy that was directed toward the fear is surrendered and now flows to the crown center. Sustained effort takes practice. If you lose your focus, start again. Keep practicing. Repeated sustained effort in self-surrendering will eventually increase your experience of star consciousness.

For some this form of meditation will come naturally; the benefits are clear and obvious. For others it may feel useless; it takes too much effort to accomplish. The benefits may not be apparent. There may even be feelings and thoughts that it's a waste of time.

Making the self-surrender meditation a regular sustained

practice without expectation of reward or benefit will go a long way toward awakening star consciousness. You will need to test it out for yourself and see. Spasmodic, fit and start practices may not lead to any "noticeable" changes. Often the changes are super-subtle.

Chapter 7 Summary:

1. Repeated sustained effort in self-remembering will eventually increase your experience of star consciousness.
2. Making the self-surrender meditation a regular sustained practice without expectation of reward or benefit will go a long way toward awakening star consciousness.

Chapter 8: Star Consciousness

Expanding consciousness will allow you to experience glimpses of star consciousness. When your psycho-logical energies of thought, feeling, desire and action come more under conscious control, you will reflect and resonate with star consciousness. You will experience physical repose, emotional calm and peace of mind.

Star consciousness is not about escape or going beyond the physical. It's more about truly committing and being in the moment and harnessing and handling energies on multiple levels – physical, psycho-logical and spiritual. Star consciousness is not psychic, metaphysical or mystical. As you evolve and expand consciousness you may have psychic experiences, mystical dreams and metaphysical mental meanderings. Be conscious of them but avoid being side tracked and overly attached to pathways that lead away from genuine star consciousness.

In order to live in star consciousness, becoming a conscious co-creator, you will need to radiate light not merely reflect it. This can come about after stepping up and taking on what the alchemists called the purificatio. This tends to be a slow, time consuming process of weeding out negative identification with negative and even obsessive thoughts, feelings, desires, and actions. Gradually, the hold they have on you diminishes. In Part 2: How to Live-Function as an Energy Being, I will offer some functional guidelines to transforming, transmuting and regenerating negative energies into higher frequency energies that are more conducive to an alignment with star consciousness.

Naturally, everybody's experience of the purificatio is different. I've been "treading the path" to star consciousness for decades. I guess I'm a slow poke. In the beginning I was in a hurry for "enlightenment." I laugh at myself now for how naïve and green I was in the first few years. Now I'm more accepting of the process and generally avoid rushing. Uprooting old habits may take a few months, many years or a lifetime(s).

Let me conclude Part 1: How to Expand Consciousness,

with a koan by the Japanese Zen Buddhist Shobogenzo:

> *When one studies Buddhism [the way to star consciousness] one studies oneself; when one studies oneself, one forgets oneself; when one forgets oneself, one is enlightened by everything and this very enlightenment breaks the bonds of clinging to both body and mind not only for oneself but for all beings as well. If the enlightenment is true, it wipes out even clinging to enlightenment, and therefore it is imperative that we return to, and live in, the world of ordinary men and women.*

Chapter 8 Summary:

1. Expanding your consciousness will allow you to experience glimpses of star consciousness.
2. Star consciousness is not about escape or going beyond the physical. It's more about truly committing to being in the moment and harnessing and handling energies on multiple levels – physical, psycho-logical and spiritual.

Part 2: How to Live-Function as an Energy Being

Chapter 1: The Frequency-Energy World

To date it is scientifically clear we live in a frequency-energy world yet most of us act like we live in a world of things. Consumer capitalism promotes, thrives and survives on the false-to-fact belief that we live-function in a materialistic thing world. We are so programmed and inoculated with the physical thing perspective we tend to reduce ourselves to sensory-bodies ignoring and excluding, for the most part, living and functioning as energy beings.

Most agree we live in a frequency-energy world. Electrical energy is mandatory to power smartphones, the internet, transportation, television, household appliances and a spectrum of other devices and technologies. The physicists, engineers, biologists, chemists and inventors who by viewing and investigating the world as energy have provided the scientifically based technologies integrated into our daily lives.

Scientists and non-scientists alike need to align their functioning with the energy-frequency world in order to be more in tune with the environment and reduce the disconnect between false-to-fact medieval thingifying and the harmonizing benefits of applying the laws of human energy to everyday living. Making the transformative transition to thinking, feeling and acting as an energy being offers a host of benefits that include experiencing greater psycho-logical equilibrium, attunement with your structural, functional purpose, drastically improving your relationships and the accessing of the wisdom to adapt to a rapidly changing world.

How do you make the transition from living as a physical being to functioning as an energy being? First, realize that it will take time. It's not like flipping a light switch. It's not instantaneous. Fundamental change doesn't happen without rigorous effort over time. Next, you must practice acting like an energy being. A major step in accomplishing this can be achieved by repeatedly reminding yourself that everything is a configuration of units of energy.

There are people who are born feeling energy. Others become conscious, awakening sensitivity to the registration of energies. There are still others who tend to be less sensitive to picking up on energies. All will benefit from learning to navigate the energy world of daily life.

Those born sensitive to feeling the vibrations of people and places often do not know that energies can be directed and managed. These empathic people usually have no training, preparation or guidance in handling the energies they feel. There's no need to convince the sensitive ones that we live in an energy world they experience. They think it is "normal" to feel the vibrations of a place and a person. Depending on how sensitive they are, they can take on the energy of a person or place often almost instantaneously.

If they have no training in handling sympathetic vibrations from people and places, they tend to think it's them. They may identify or associate a psycho-logical negative feeling with a health issue like a headache, anxiety attack or a stomach pain, etc. They may sense-feel a person or place as a positive energy. This can be energizing in a way that gets them over excited, over amped and/or started down a path that may seem appealing at first but actually gets them side-tracked from their genuine, structural direction.

Many who are not born energy aware often go through a difficult life challenge that leads to a heightened conscious experience. Conscious energy tends to increase sensitivity to feeling the vibrations of people and places. Once a person commits to becoming more conscious through diligent daily effort then learning to navigate the energy-frequency world is necessary in order to handle positive and negative energies.

Those who are unaware and tend not to feel the energies from people and places can still benefit from knowing how to direct, manage and transform their energies. I've been in a place that feels draining and exhausting. From time to time I'll ask a less sensitive one who is in that place, "Do you feel that?" Often, they will reply, "No, what? I don't feel anything." Then I'll think to myself, 'how is that possible?' It's obvious, even overwhelming to me.

One of the ways you can be more conscious and selective of the energies you give attention to is a rudimentary understanding of the Hindu gunas or qualities. They are labeled tamas, rajas and sattva. As you go about your day, the three guna spectrums of energy impact your energy-field influencing your psycho-logical, physiological state.

The gunas are essentially three frequency wavebands. Tamas energies are vibratory qualities tending toward a lower frequency. These include but are not limited to emotional negativity, depression, gross foods, dark energy places and unconscious low energy people. Rajas energies include positive feelings, passionate interests and daily routine activities. Sattva energies tend to be more refined including higher frequency qualities that include uplifting and inspiring people and places, creativity, and nature.

As a functioning energy being you will want to pay careful attention to which of the three guna qualities you are giving your attention. If you are indulging feelings of hate, depression, negativity and fear then you will be unbalanced toward the tamas end of the guna spectrum. The excessive self-centeredness generated by tamas qualities will usually reduce the rajas and sattva energies experienced. The conscious cultivation of sattva energies increases uplifting creative and spiritual qualities. When you give more of your attention to thoughtful, kind, creative and compassionate pursuits the dark cloud of excessive tamas dissipates.

Regardless of increasing sattva and reducing tamas, you direct your attention in a positive way to rajas as well. Purposeful action is one of the most constructive raja qualities. Random, directionless, non-purposeful action may generate excitement but will move you about from impulse to impulse much like a boat without a rudder. Positive sattva will improve your energy level.

You want to avoid as much as possible draining your energy and devitalizing yourself by lowering your energy. It may lead to lowering your immune system and opening yourself up to health issues. Along these lines, doing too much can exhaust you and doing too little, being lazy-inert, can lower the vitality of a strong immune system. Too much 'bad' or too much 'good' can be devitalizing.

Stabilizing as a functional energy being demands self-monitoring by practicing self-remembering, self-reflection and self-observation. Abandoning yourself to unconscious, compulsive thoughts, feelings and actions that resonate with negative tamas and rajas will tip the scales toward unbalanced guna qualities, preventing the alignment with clear and stable star consciousness.

Reading and learning "about" the energy world provides a verbal map but having a map without taking the journey accomplishes little. When you are conscious in the moment you tend to continuously create a relatively accurate map of the moment to moment energy conditions. As a result, you tend to navigate the energy world making adjustments to the ever-changing energies.

Because of cultural-educational beliefs and values, many identify knowing with having a concept, idea or verbal map. I use the word knowing here with the conscious and flexible skill of making functional adjustments to the current energy conditions.

Listening to the weather forecast can give you a fairly accurate verbal map of the day's weather. However, if you mistake the forecast for the actual weather conditions, it can misinform in a mild uncomfortable way ranging to a drastic life-threatening event. For example, if the weather forecast predicts it to be sunny and you step outside and there are ominous storm clouds, are you going to cling to the verbal map of sunny or let go and deal with the present storm clouds? Similarly, if you mentally accept that you live in an energy world but do not practice navigating the energy world, then you may know the way intellectually, but you really do not function as an energy being.

Haphazardly practicing directing and managing your

energy will not accomplish becoming a fully functioning energy being. It's a skill that takes daily, hourly, minute-to-minute and ultimately second-to-second practice. Becoming an energy being is a process through a continuum from beginner, intermediate and eventually to a master level.

There are encouraging signs in the educational system. In recent years, there has been a movement away from solely memorizing information to actually achieving competency. This is often brought about by what's called project-based learning (PBL). PBL addresses and solves real life problems and then shares the findings in a public forum. Knowing and memorizing how to become a functioning energy being may be informative and interesting but will not transform you in a way that unfolds the possibility of star consciousness.

Chapter 1: Summary

1. To date it is scientifically clear we live in a frequency-energy world yet most of us act like we live in a world of things.
2. We are so programmed and inoculated with the physical thing perspective we tend to reduce ourselves to sensory-bodies ignoring and excluding, for the most part, living and functioning as energy beings.
3. Scientists and non-scientists alike need to align their functioning with the energy-frequency world in order to be more in tune with the environment and reduce the disconnect between false-to-fact medieval thingifying and the harmonizing benefits of applying the laws of human energy to everyday living.
4. Making the transformation to thinking, feeling and acting as an energy being offers a host of benefits that include experiencing greater psycho-logical equilibrium, attunement with your structural, functional purpose, drastically improving your relationships and the accessing of the wisdom to adapt to a rapidly changing world.
5. Conscious energy tends to increase sensitivity to feeling

the vibrations of people, places and things.
6. You want to avoid as much as possible draining your energy and devitalizing yourself by lowering your energy.
7. Stabilizing as a functional energy being demands the self-monitoring by practicing self-remembering, self-reflection and self-observation.
8. I use the word knowing here with the mutable skill of making functional adjustments to the ever-changing energies.
9. Becoming an energy being is a process through a continuum from beginner, intermediate and eventually to a master level.

Chapter 2: Positive, Negative, Neutral Energies

At one time I worked for a multinational financial corporation. The local office was managed by a man who, when he did not like what you did, was verbally abusive. The negative energy was an unpleasant experience to say the least.

Maintaining a positive energy in the face of these attacks usually proved to be difficult. The effect was intense and triggered emotional reactions that tended to pull me into a negative emotional spiral. Fighting back by verbally retaliating usually resulted in more negativity. The power of positive thinking was useless. What could be done to handle the energy?

I remembered the story of the man who hurled insults at the Buddha. No matter how abusive the insults the Buddha remained unmoved. The story goes that the Buddha asked the man, "If someone offers you a gift and you decline to accept it to whom then does it belong?" The man responded, "Then it belongs to the person who offered it." Buddha smiled, "That's correct. So, if I decline to accept your abuse does it not then belong to you?" The man walked away speechless.

The Buddha accessed neutral energy. He registered the negative insults but did not react. Like water off a duck's back the Buddha did not react or accept the insults. Where then does the energy go? It stays with the insulter.

I decided to give it a try. I reminded myself to not take the manager's attacks personally, to register but not react. When he verbally attacked, I went into neutral. By going into neutral I did not take on the negative energy. The negative energy he put out described a circuit back into the manager.

Honestly, for me it was not as easy as it might sound. It took concentration, mindfulness and willingness to not justify and rationalize. Yes, at first, I felt compelled to defend myself or retaliate. With practice I improved the going into neutral skill.

Eventually, I noticed the number of verbal attacks were reduced to a minimum. The negative anger energy made him feel uneasy. Instead of me taking on the energy it boomeranged back into him.

In order to become a functional energy being it will necessitate you becoming adept at handling positive, negative and neutral energies. Practicing physical repose, emotional calm and peace of mind means accessing neutral energies. You are neither for nor against. You flexibly center yourself in the eye of the storm. You remain unmoved by both positive complements and negative insults.

Energy follows attention. When you give less attention to a person, place or thing it receives less energy. When you give more attention to a person, place or thing it receives more energy. Seems obvious, right? But can you control the direction of energy from second to second?

When your interest level is minimal then your attention weakens. Thoughts, feelings, desires and actions receive less energy. When your interest level is heightened and sustained, thoughts, feelings, desires and actions collect more energy.

As a functional energy being you will have more choices as you become more conscious on who, what and where you focus your attention. Accepting and settling for unconscious living more or less dooms you to repeat an endless circuit of thoughts, feelings, desires and actions. Vitvan worded it this way: "Everything describes a circuit. If it wasn't for a circuit, we'd have no light. Nature works according to those circuits, natural order. Once the creative force is kindled it is deaf, dumb and blind. It knows only one thing, to fulfill its circuit. No matter what you think about, it is a current [energy] trying to fulfill its circuit."

When you are conscious, and you go into neutral you activate the thalamal-cortical gap. The automatic thoughts, feelings, desires and actions may potentially be non-identified with by giving them less attention, value and energy. Accessing the thalamal-cortical gap is like counting to 10 when experiencing compulsive anger, fear and/or desire. There's a pause, a gap. In this gap you give yourself the opportunity to direct your energy into neutral.

As you will discover if you persist, if you haven't

already, energy provides opportunities and choices for change. A functioning human-energy being sees, accepts and handles what is. Living in past behavior patterns tends to repel conscious neutral energy. You are habit bound. Vitvan: "Once the creative force is kindled, it is deaf, dumb and blind."

Self-reflect on where you focus your attention. If you are not focused in the moment you will more than likely be placing your attention on the past or future. Past memories will usually be positive or negative. Possibilities and plans for the future will usually be positive or negative. Being mindful in the moment, in a state of wordless awareness, accesses the flow of neutral energy.

Learning to *go into neutral* takes time, keen awareness and practical application. By noticing your automatic likes and dislikes, you'll begin to see you are conditioned to a two-valued orientation where likes are positive, and dislikes are negative.

Going into neutral entails you to suspend attachments to likes and dislikes resulting in alternative possibilities. *Going into neutral* presents more conscious choices. The two-valued orientation limits thinking and acting to a world of opposites.

Have you ever been caught up in a situation where you insist on being right? Sometimes being "right" is critical for avoiding a life challenge or even a disaster. If you know taking a road that will head you into an extensive traffic delay or a long detour, you may be right to take another route. Other times being "right" is not critical and, in fact, can exasperate a situation into a conflict from minor arguments to major wars. Let's say a friend points to a rock and says it's brown. To you it's clearly not brown but tan. Do you compulsively have to be right? Or can you let go your "rightness" and say to the friend, "Yeah, I see what you mean."

Letting go of the two-valued orientation can be a monumental task for some. It only takes a second to get and accept the idea. But to be vigilant in uprooting the deeply planted habit of good-bad, right-wrong, happy-sad, hope-despair, win-lose, etc. is not instantaneous. Neutral energy releases and flows each time you move through, passed and beyond the opposites, enjoying the freedom and inner space and peace provided by not having to win or be right.

Former U. S. Senator from California, S.I. Hayakawa, often used an example of a two-valued orientation that potentially resulted in death. During World War II patrols and guards around military perimeters asked when they encountered someone, "friend or foe?" If no satisfactory answer was given, guards were entitled to open fire.

Hayakawa summarized the two-valued orientation as follows:

Two-valued orientation is a widespread, and often misleading, form of simplification in which language is used to represent reality in limited, binary terms regardless of intermediary nuances. The danger resides in the reduction of a complex reality to a simple binary contrast (e.g. yes/no for/against), which is easily adopted and abandoned and may discourage further discernment. IT IS NOT just two different or opposite opinions, but rather a manifestation of a thought-system that leaves no alternative to a binary view of reality.

Chapter 2: Summary

1. In order to become a functional energy being it will necessitate you becoming adept at handling positive, negative and neutral energies.
2. Energy follows attention. When you give less attention to a person, place or thing it receives less energy.
3. As a functional energy being you will have more choices as you become more conscious on who, what and where you focus your attention.
4. A functioning human-energy being sees, accepts and handles what is.
5. Being mindful in the moment, in a state of wordless awareness, accesses the flow of neutral energy.

6. Neutral energy releases and flows each time you move through, passed and beyond the opposites, enjoying the freedom and inner peace provided by not having to win or be right.

Chapter 3: Non-Identification

Have you ever been stopped behind a bus in city traffic? You cannot see what's happening up ahead. Your vision is blocked by the height of the bus. You remain at a standstill. You might have a mental-emotional reaction blaming the bus driver for the delay.

When traffic eventually moves again, and you drive by the delay point you find out that the delay was the result of construction. The bus driver was stopped because of the construction not because he or she was an inattentive driver. Your false-to-fact identification triggered a reaction. Frustration, anger, exasperation, impatience, hostility, etc. psycho-logical energies were identified with.

For many years Walter Cronkite, the anchor for CBS television network news, signed off the broadcast by saying, "And that's the way it is." Cronkite's news director tried to convince him not to say it because obviously in a fifteen-minute newscast you cannot cover all the day's news. Clearly, it's not the way it is.

At the heart of identification is (ha, ha) the is of identity. Habitual false-to-fact identifications may have long lasting psycho-logical problems and, often culminate in non-survival, self-destructive behaviors. Alfred Korzybski, author of *Science and Sanity*, wrote, "This 'emery' in the nervous system I call identification. It involves deeply rooted 'principles' which are invariably false-to-facts and so our orientation based on them cannot lead to adjustments and sanity."

Transforming from an unconscious sense-based person to a conscious functioning energy being is largely a process of noticing your automatic identifications and then practicing non-identification. As a result, you no longer give them value cutting off the energy that sustains them. One of the most deeply rooted habitual identifications is the identification with your "body." It appears evident, obvious, true, fundamental, etc. So, why question it?

Korzybski answered this when he wrote, "Identification represents, an affective tension, the mildest semantic disturbance, consisting of an error in meanings and evaluations." Expanding your consciousness will guide you to seeing that you often identify with images, thoughts, concepts, feelings, desires, memories, etc. that are not accurate. Consequently, accepting them as accurate and then acting on them will undoubtedly compound conflicts, problems and needless dramas.

Non-identification frees you from the invisible constraints that stifle consciousness. Experiencing the liberating non-identification that you are not only a "body" but vastly more, opens up a dynamic world of energies that can be directed, managed and transformed. As you gradually withdraw false-to-fact identifications, you mine energies that have been dammed up for years, even a lifetime(s).

One of the most pernicious and delusional identifications is attempting to reason with an unreasonable person. As you expand consciousness, you base more of your life decisions on valuable and valid reasons. They make sense; they are verifiable by perceptive awareness and registration of energies.

The energy experiences are so apparent to you that you may have a tendency to believe others will be as reasonable as you. You make the miscalculation that if you simple verbalize the reason the other person will see what you see. Simple, right?

If the other person has not committed to and practiced expanding consciousness in the functional ways mapped out in Part 1, they will not comprehend what you're talking about. Typically, they mistakenly believe they are reasonable. In fact, they will often believe they are more reasonable than you. They may attempt to change your mind by convincing you of your wayward ways.

If you have a friend, co-worker or life partner who has wholly identified with unconsciousness, then you may not be able to sustain a reciprocal relationship. It may be wise for you to avoid explanations, the sharing of insights, attempting to reason, etc. in favor of acceptance, compassion, patience and understanding.

We function on different levels. This doesn't mean there are "superior" or "inferior" levels in the sense that a more conscious one is superior-better and less conscious one is inferior-worse. The more conscious you become the more respectful you are of each person's lifepath. We each learn in our own way and in our own time.

One method of differentiating consciousness stages was introduced by Alfred Korzybski in his book *Science and Sanity*. He presented four functional levels of consciousness. They are:
- One-valued orientation
- Two-valued orientation
- Three-valued orientation
- Infinite-valued orientation

The one-valued orientation is based on a relatively fixed belief system that a person accepts wholeheartedly. The belief system, therefore, doesn't need changing or adapting as an adjustment to the present life circumstances. This orientation tends to be non-scientific and even anti-scientific.

The two-valued orientation described earlier recognizes that there is at least two points of view. They recognize there may be an opposite perspective. Usually they do not agree with it. They tend to experience the world on a dualistic verbal level: good-bad, right-wrong, light-dark, black-white, right-wrong, happy-sad, etc. Living in the two-valued orientation attracts conflicts, disagreements and strife.

The three-valued orientation relies on authority rather than on present consciousness. The expert knows best. They have the credentials like doctor, lawyer, general, teacher, scientist, etc. When the authority says such and such, blah-blah-blah, the three-valued oriented person accepts what the authority claims to be valid. Their range of consciousness is wider than the one and two valued orientations but limited compared to the infinite-valued orientation.

A person with the infinite-valued orientation functions, more or less, as an energy being. They are aware that the energy world changes constantly. They value being conscious in the moment and practice expanding their consciousness. By self-remembering they recognize when they go unconscious and are not in the present. Consequently, while unaware their decisions and choices tend not to be based on non-verbal energy-frequency circumstances.

Here are two stories that underscore the importance of non-identification, the infinite-valued orientation and being in the moment.

I lived on the second floor of a duplex that had a stairway leading to the entrance. When it snowed, I took the precaution of sweeping the snow off the stairs and spreading salt crystals. This made it safe to climb up and down the stairs.

One time after it snowed I swept the stairs and spread the salt. I "thought" it was safe. After all, the precautions worked "before." I "thought" and "worked before" indicated I was not in the moment. I was going by the past.

When I stepped on the top step to walk down to the ground level, I slipped on the black ice that had formed on the top stair. The salt crystals had not worked its way through the black ice. Fortunately, I did not get hurt except for a bruised ego. I slid down the stairs on my butt like a slapstick comedy actor. I was surprised, concerned for my safety and laughing to myself all at the same time.

I realized almost immediately I had not paid attention in the moment to the condition of the top stair. I automatically assumed it was safe like all the other past times. Practicing conscious non-identification for years does not always make you conscious. You must remain ever vigilant. It took less than a second to identify with the past. My mental map was not accurate to the territory.

Once I was stopped at a red light at a busy intersection. I was one of two drivers positioned in the front waiting for the light to turn green. The driver to my left was eager to get through the intersection, edging forward. I was more or less in the moment practicing non-identification. I was neither eager nor non-eager.

The light turned green. The driver to my left gassed it. I paused for a second or two. A car coming from the left ran the red light crashing into the driver's car who was in a hurry. Luckily no one was severely injured. I was grateful that I, in a sense, made my own luck by paying attention. What a lesson in the value of non-identification.

Chapter 3: Summary

1. Habitual false-to-fact identifications may have long lasting psycho-logical problems and often culminate in non-survival, self-destructive behaviors.
2. Non-identification frees you from the invisible constraints that stifle consciousness.
3. The more conscious you become the more respectful you are of each person's lifepath. We each learn in our own way and in our own time.
4. A person with an infinite-valued orientation functions, more or less, as an energy being.
5. Practicing conscious non-identification for years does not always make you conscious. You must be ever vigilant.

Chapter 4: Rhythmic Alternation

Listening to a bird song, watching the rising and setting of the sun or touching the knit weave of a scarf, speak of what has often been called heaven's first law, rhythmic alternation. The ups and downs of joy and sorrow, hardship and happiness, love and hate are poles of the life activity battery. Without the ever-alternating rhythm between positive and negative life loses its vitality. It takes the rubbing, the friction, the conflict to ignite the fires of action, thought and feeling which eventually manifests as events, relationships and creativity.

In most areas of our present-day lifestyles we witness the alternation between opposites from the simple example of leaving home in the morning to returning at night, to the more complex national and international alternations between war and peace. In all our institutions: business, government, medicine, home, media, military, arts, agriculture and education, rhythmic alternation takes place whether we are aware of it or not. Just as the microscopic atom maintains its delicate structure because of the dynamic balance of forces between the electrons and the protons so do our institutions survive as long as they maintain some kind of balance between ups and downs, progress and retrogression. Unfortunately, to date we do not thoroughly understand and apply the principle of rhythmic alternation to our institutions.

When we become over-attached, focused or preoccupied with the positive ups and negative downs, we tend to lose our equilibrium and natural rhythm. All of us have, at one time or other, lost our footing while climbing a stairway. Usually we're overjoyed about something, depressed, in a hurry or intoxicated. We lose our balance momentarily and in that instant the possibility of injury is increased.

Even the athlete, who for only a second loses his or her balance, timing and rhythm risks the possibility of defeat. The musician, who performs a solo for a philharmonic orchestra, loses his or her rhythm and plays off key, spoils the mood and tone of the entire piece. And when we fail to apply rhythmic alternation to our institutions, they begin to crumble.

The lesson we need to learn from the natural law of rhythmic alternation is threefold. One, we must see and then know that all life is rhythmic. Two, we must observe ourselves and see where we are not rhythmic. And three, we must make an effort to find our natural rhythm so that we don't injure ourselves physically, psychologically and/or spiritually. Number three is perhaps the most important of all since without some change in ourselves as individuals there is little chance of change in the social fabric, including our institutions.

A conscious effort toward living rhythmically must include watching how we channel our life energy. There are four basic areas where our energy is channeled: intellectual, feeling, physical and desire. None of these are "pure" channels; they each intermingle with the other. But if we can determine which areas we channel most of our energy, we can attempt to consciously alternate and channel our energy in another complementary direction.

For example, if you have an active intellect, you can balance by participating in some physical activity where you're more focused on the body and things instead of words and ideas. Or, if you're too much into feeling, love, the arts and music, you might balance by acknowledging your desires, drives for material possessions, food and pleasures.

Living more in harmony with nature, human structures and the cosmos by functioning according to the law of rhythmic alternation, the horizons of the future open like fields of wild spring flowers. But if we remain non-rhythmic, becoming fixated to one pole or another, we lose our footing and trip up in some unlikely way.

As we go about our daily duties and chores fulfilling responsibilities and obligations, we must avoid as much as possible every stress and strain. When our thinking and feeling become more rhythmic, our actions must follow less we throw ourselves off balance again. By putting into practice the principle of least resistance we gain great economy of time and energy. When tension builds from over pressure either at home or at work, we should remind ourselves that we've lost our rhythm once again and in order to regain it nothing helps more than following the line of least resistance.

Before taking any action from getting out of bed to washing the dishes, mentally anticipate each act in the process of execution. For example, take getting out of a chair. In order to follow the line of least resistance, first let go of the tension in the stomach, neck and back. Then, leaning forward from the hip joint in a swift swiveling motion, allow yourself to stand without clutching every muscle.

Mountain climbers are particularly knowledgeable about economy of action. Some years ago, in the mid-1960s, I had the opportunity to learn mountain climbing in the Grand Tetons of Wyoming. My teacher, Glenn Exum, was a mountain man in appearance, reputation and in action. As a climber at age 60, he was still formidable; something hard to believe until you saw how he climbed.

Most of the young people in my class were in their teens and early twenties; ready and eager to make the ascent. Mr. Exum gathered us together and told us right off that if we wanted to climb we must learn economy of action and rhythmic motion. That didn't make sense to most of us until later on up the trail to the climbing area. As we started up the trail, he suggested we walk deliberately picking each spot and stepping firmly, lightly and consciously.

Well, that lasted about 5 minutes. He was too slow for us. Instead, we all raced right by him, telling him we'd meet him at the base of the mountain. Before we were three-quarters of the way, we stopped to rest. We were already exhausted. After a few minutes, Mr. Exum, with a smile on his face and his gait steady and rhythmic, hiked on by us.

As a climber, Mr. Exum was a master of the principle of least resistance. Despite his years, he could hike and climb for hours without a rest because he did not waste energy rushing, wanting to get to the summit all at once. Just as diligently as Mr.

Exum conserved his energy in climbing, we all must conserve our energy throughout our day whether climbing stairs, cooking or working at our desk. In this way, we cultivate rhythmic alternation.

A couple of aides to learning and establishing economy in the use of your energy include singing, humming and breathing. While you work, keep time by singing or humming. Also, when out walking inhale slowly and steadily as you take six steps, then hold the breath as you pace three steps; then exhale gradually as you walk six steps, hold baited breath while you pace three steps, etc. You can increase or decrease the number of steps until you find the count that is easiest; but always concentrating on the rhythm.

By applying the principle of least resistance to simple daily activities, we gain our natural rhythm as well as extra energy so valuable and necessary if we desire to fulfill our potential during our short stay on this earth. Glenn Exum taught me that taking it slow, step by step, can be the fastest way to the top of the mountain.

Chapter 4: Summary

1. When we become over-attached, focused or preoccupied with the positive ups and downs, we tend to lose our equilibrium and natural rhythm.
2. A conscious effort toward living rhythmically must include watching how we channel our life energy.
3. By putting into practice the principle of least resistance we gain great economy of time and energy.
4. By applying the principle of least resistance to simple daily activities, we gain our natural rhythm as well as extra energy so valuable and necessary if we desire to fulfill our potential during our short stay on earth.

Chapter 5: Resonance, Reflection, Rapports

What is resonance? Let's take the example of two highly tuned violins. Place one violin on a table and play a note on the other. Observe carefully the same string on the un-played violin. Notice that it's vibrating yet it hasn't been played. There's a resonance between the two violin notes/strings.

What's going on? When drawing the bow over a violin string, the string vibrates at its natural frequency. Since both violins are precisely tuned both strings vibrate at the same natural frequency. The acoustical energy in the form of air waves from the played violin impinges on the un-played violin since they share the same natural frequency.

Why is understanding resonance essential to functioning as an energy being? Whatever you think, feel, desire, say, emote and do is like plucking a note on a violin. A vibration is emitted and emanated that will resonate with the same frequency thoughts, feelings, desires, words, emotions and actions.

Ask yourself, "What am I resonating with?" When you are happy, compassionate, joyful and thoughtful, you resonate with others who experience these natural frequencies. When you are unhappy, cold-hearted, dissatisfied and thoughtless, you will resonate with others who experience these frequencies. Becoming more conscious of what and who you're resonating with affords an opportunity to choose wisely.

In order to function as an energy being you must choose more and more who and what makes you happy, compassionate, joyful and thoughtful. Then you will develop the skill and wisdom to better direct, manage and transform your life energy resulting in a greater resonance with star consciousness.

Becoming more conscious increases your sensitivity to registering and feeling energies. In a sense, you become a human reflector of whatever and whoever you are around physically and psychically. Have you ever traveled to another country? The psycho-logical energies are different than the psycho-logical energies in your home country. You see and sense those different energies and call them French, Tibetan, Australian, American, etc.

In a way, whatever and whoever you reflect becomes who you are on a personality level, especially if you reflect unconsciously. You acquire beliefs, attitudes, habits, language, speech patterns, traditions, etc. that "make" you a human from a certain place and time.

Earlier in this book you read about self-reflection. Expanding consciousness involves self-reflection. Additionally, expanding consciousness requires knowing that whatever and whoever you resonate with can be reflected and absorbed into your mental-emotional-physical auric-field. As a consequence you learn to be highly discriminative of what and who you reflect. Your psyche, your auric-energy-field can ripple like water on a placid lake with whatever and whoever you direct attentions, interests and likes.

Space telescopes have the most sensitive reflective mirrors. They can reflect star light from billions of light years. If you aspire in a natural, deeper psycho-logical way to star consciousness, you will want to reflect spiritual frequencies more and unconscious limiting frequencies less.

The Hubble space telescope had a design flaw in the mirrors that distorted the light from deep space. After careful analysis, the scientists discovered the mirror design was off by only one millimeter. That's less than the thickness of most coins. As you get to know yourself, you discover and eliminate the design flaws that distort star consciousness.

Vitvan clarifies what a rapport is in his book *Healing Technic*. He writes, "One cannot register frequencies of another unless a circuit is established. This circuit is labeled a "rapport." The circuit is established by synchronization of what we might designate one's rate of vibration in correspondence or co-response with that of another."

A functioning energy being is motivated to be conscious of the rapports experienced, felt, picked up on from people, places and things. Not all headaches, migraines, gas attacks, stomach pains, eye troubles, heart palpitations, etc. are disease symptoms. You need to sharply discriminate physiological maladies from psycho-logical rapports.

When you cut the current from a circuit you will no longer resister the rapport. Test this scientifically. Next time you feel sharp intermittent pains in the solar plexus or when you first feel a headache coming on, choose not to identify with the pain. Let it go. Do not give it your attention. Avoid labeling it with words like "I have a headache," "I have a stomach ache" etc.

Instead, begin slow rhythmic breathing through the nose to the count of three in and then to the count of three out. Keep this up. Simultaneously, practice going into neutral. Refuse to identify intensely with the negative vibration you are registering. Automatic sustained identification will provide the rapport with more energy. If the stomach pain goes away, the headache subsides, the gas attack disappears after redirecting attention-energy from the disturbance, then you very well may have been experiencing a rapport.

Ask yourself these questions. Where do I spend my time? Who do I regularly interact with? Pay attention to the energy qualities of friends, family and co-workers. Before connecting more deeply with new acquaintances, note the thoughts, feelings, speech, desires, actions of that person. There's an interchange and intermingling of energies between people. As a conscious functioning energy being you are responsible for knowing the quality of frequencies between yourself and others.

Here's a tip that can assist you in avoiding and/or reducing negative rapports. If a person behaves unconsciously, in other words, shows no or minimal self-remembering, self-observation, self-reflection, seriously consider not cultivating a relationship. Find a way to excuse yourself rather than getting intertwined in a lengthy conversation or having to spend excessive time around their unconscious, self-centered energies.

Chapter 5: Summary
1. Whatever you think, feel, desire, say, emote and do is like plucking a note on a violin. A vibration is emitted and emanated that will resonate with the same frequency thoughts, feelings, desires, words, emotions and actions.
2. In order to function as an energy being you must choose more and more who and what makes you happy, compassionate, joyful and thoughtful.
3. You acquire beliefs, attitudes, habits, language, speech patterns, traditions, etc. that "make" you a human from a certain place and time.
4. If you aspire in a natural, deeper psycho-logical way to star consciousness, you will want to reflect spiritual frequencies more and unconscious limiting frequencies less.
5. As a conscious functioning energy being you are responsible for knowing the quality of frequencies between yourself and others.

Chapter 6: Automatic Energies

We depend on the functioning of automatic energies instinctively, emotionally and mentally. Mostly these energies are self-acting. In other words, we do not consciously direct and maintain their activities. Nevertheless, we as conscious energy beings can be aware of their operation and choose to cooperate by responding to their natural requirements.

The instinctual automatic energies include, hunger, thirst, heartbeat, breathing, digestion, sense-functioning, sleep and reflex movements. Mastering your energies calls for being attuned to the natural inclinations of the instincts.

There's a story of the Zen master Bankei, teaching at the Ryumon Temple. A Shinshu priest listening to Bankei became jealous of his large audience. The priest rudely interrupted Bankei boasting, "The founder of our sect had such miraculous powers that he held a pencil in his hand on one bank of the river, his attendant held up a paper on the other bank, and the teacher wrote the holy name of Amida through the air. Can you do such a wonderful thing?"

Bankei replied calmly, "Perhaps your fox can perform that trick, but that is not the way of Zen. For me, it's wonderful when I feel hungry, I eat, and when I feel thirsty, I drink."

As you expand consciousness into becoming a functioning energy being, you will naturally acknowledge instinctive signals of hunger and thirst. Keeping life simple and avoiding egocentric demonstrations of physical, psychic and mental powers, will propel you toward star consciousness. Until the advent of the 21st century and the rise of digital technologies, automatic energies were usually kept private. Unless you were an empath, you were not aware of another's instinctual, emotional and/or mental activities. For millennia the emphasis was on keeping these automatic energies to oneself. Cultural beliefs, values, mores, customs and traditions often gave rise to and reinforced privacy, saving face, secretiveness, keeping a poker face, etc.

Today technologies know what you're internally experiencing. Exercise machines monitor your heart rate, smartphone apps track the distance you walk each day and ubiquitous cameras capture actions and words otherwise kept private. Neuroscientist Poppy Crum gave a TED talk where she said, "Technology has become incredibly intelligent and already knows a lot about our internal states." During the talk she gave four examples of current technologies that peer into, expose or makes you aware of your inner automatic energies. Dr. Crum calls them "empathetic technologies."

The four she mentions in the talk are micro-expressions, pupil dilation, infrared thermal imaging and breath chemistry. Micro-expressions can be detected by a computer software program that measures the slightest changes in facial expressions. It can tell the difference, for instance, between a real smile and a fake one. The autonomic nervous system drives your pupils to dilate and contract based on your cognitive effort. Crum says, "We know this from neuroscience." The pupil doesn't lie. It is truly a window to the internal workings of the brain-mind continuum.

Changes in body temperature radiate an energy that can be seen in the infrared light spectrum. These thermal images show the reds as hotter and the blues as cooler. Crum says, "The dynamic signature of our thermal response gives away our changes in stress, how hard our brain is working, whether we're paying attention and engaged in the conversation we might be having and even whether we're experiencing a picture of fire as if it were real."

The fourth empathic technology measures the chemical composition of the breath revealing our feelings. Crum installed carbon dioxide detectors throughout the TED talk theater capable of measuring precisely the CO_2 concentrations in the room. She then played the same video clip with two different soundtracks. An image of a man standing at a window has an audio of eerie music followed by a woman screaming. The same video played with cheerful music and a woman laughing. As you might have guessed the CO_2 levels went up with the first suspenseful clip and went down with the more joyful soundtrack. Crum emphasizes, "We broadcast a chemical signature of our emotions."

Vitvan in his book *The Seven Initiations* echoes Crum's research. Letting go of sensed-based objective identifications eliminates feeling ashamed, living in self-censorship and caring about the opinions of others. You realize you are an "illuminated billboard." Thus, you work to eliminate and transmute the negative content of the psyche.

What is an emotion? It is an automatic visceral reaction to a person, place, event, word, image or thing. Some emotional reactions are low on the emotional Richter scale; others are more seismic. A highly functioning energy being is conscious of the scope of emotional reactions and learns to register but not react, transforming emotional energies into fuel for evolving star consciousness.

While attending the University of Nevada pursuing a doctorate in education, I heard about an opportunity to study Spanish in Costa Rica during the summer break. I applied, was accepted and enrolled in a Spanish language college in Puntarenas, Costa Rica located on a Pacific Ocean beach. My emotional reactions were positive and eager, anticipating a wonderful experience.

Before leaving I needed to make sure I was enrolled for the fall semester. I met with an enrollment counselor in order to get that done. At the end of the meeting he assured me I was enrolled for fall. Everything was taken care of.

A couple of weeks later while studying Spanish in Costa Rica I received an email from the university warning me that if I didn't enroll by a certain date I would miss the fall semester and lose my scholarship. A seismic emotional reaction registered high in the Richter scale. I was consumed by emotional energies. The gap between what I believed to be the case and what was now apparently a new circumstance opened an uncontrolled emotional eruption.

Anger, fear, revenge, despair, depression, hatred, etc. flowed like molten emotional lava. I was up all night gripped by the emotional fire storm. I made up numerous negative scenarios. I plotted how I would sue the enrollment counselor and get him fired. The fear of the unknown possibilities had me wondering what I was going to do.

The next morning, thoroughly drained and exhausted, I walked along the beach to school. The front desk person said hello and asked me how I was doing. Buenos dias, Como esta? I told her what happened. She responded by saying she would look into for me. After class I stopped back to see her. She informed me that the problem was solved. The email had been a mistake.

What a lesson. Register but don't react. Pause. Count to ten. Breath. It's wise to harness your automatic emotional energies. I'm fortunate that the angel receptionist helped me. If I had acted on my delirious insanity, I may have jeopardized enjoying Costa Rica and my studies by doing something reckless and regrettable.

Automatic emotional energies cannot be separated from automatic mental energies. The intense emotional reaction I identified with and experienced in Costa Rica was fed by uncontrolled mental energies. Have you ever been up at night 'thinking?' When you practice self-observation and self-reflection take careful notice of what you automatically are thinking about. Do you think in words? Do you think in images? Do you think about work, relationships, family, health, pressing problems, etc.

Here's a thought. You can choose not to think automatically. You can choose not to identify with the often obsessive automatic thinking. The fundamental law of human energy is energy follows attention. If you focus on the facts, the structures, functions and orders of what you are thinking about, then the stream of words and images that automatically arise and fall away in the mental field have less of a hold on you.

What if I had gathered facts after receiving the email that I was not enrolled for the fall semester? What if I asked some questions to help me gather the facts? Who sent the email? Was the email a mistake? How could I verify that the email was accurate? Did I have documentation that confirmed I was indeed enrolled?

Structured, functional and ordered thinking based on the facts reduces the wasted energy generated by negative, automatic mental-emotional thinking. Often, we falsely believe if we think long and hard about something we will miraculously figure out the answer. More often than not you are better off not attempting to figure something out. Try letting it go. Directing your attention away from automatic thinking, can free you from being drained and exhausted. This may allow the facts to present themselves through serendipity, synchronicity and intuition.

Chapter 6: Summary

1. Keeping life simple and avoiding egocentric demonstrations of physical, psychic and mental powers will propel you toward star consciousness.
2. You realize you are an illumined billboard. Thus, you work to eliminate and transmute the negative content of the psyche.
3. A highly functioning energy being is conscious of the scope of emotional reactions and learns to register but not react, transforming emotional energies into fuel for evolving star consciousness.
4. Structured, functional and ordered thinking based on the facts reduces the wasted energy generated by negative, automatic mental-emotional thinking.
5. Directing your attention away from automatic thinking, can free you from being drained and exhausted. This may allow the facts to present themselves through serendipity, synchronicity and intuition.

Chapter 7: Relating Energies

Getting to know how you think, feel, emote, desire, speak and act leads naturally to knowing how others think feel, emote, desire, speak and act. It will become apparent to you that there are three fundamental energies in every relationship. Those three energies are: Energy 1 – what's going on energetically with you, Energy 2 – what's going on energetically with another, and Energy 3 – what are the energies resonating, radiating and absorbing between you and another.

Generally, when a person remains unconscious and lacks self-knowledge they are blind or unaware of energies 2 and 3. Their focus and attention is on what's going on with them, not on an energy level, but more on what they want for themselves. Those wants are usually materialistic and desire-driven. Others, they unconsciously assume, are there to give them what they want. Or, put another way, they think, 'how can I get what I want' from them.

It is imperative as an evolving energy being you recognize those in your day to day life who are blind to energies 2 and 3. There's a tendency to project our state of being on others. This will usually end up releasing a negative exchange of energies. Projection means you are not clearly registering the other's energies. You are deaf, dumb and blind to energies 2 and 3.

Here's an example of a negative exchange of energies. A young man I knew in his early twenties committed to and practiced expanding consciousness. In the early phases of becoming conscious there's a tendency to want to spread the word. He met a woman who mirrored his enthusiasm and interest but in reality, she just liked the idea of being more conscious. She did not practice being conscious.

He was not functional yet as an energy being; usually it's a minimum three to five-year introductory process. He mistook the projected image of the woman for is "soul-mate." He "fell in love" and married her. It turned out to be a volatile, drama-driven relationship. Eventually, it was so toxic that it ended in a nasty divorce.

As a functioning energy being it's mandatory you withdraw projections. Projections are emotionally charged images in the mind that distort, fabricate and fantasize. When you project you are not in the moment, you are not registering the energy from the other person or energy from between you and the other person.

Dr. Robert Johnson, author of *WE: Understanding the Psychology of Romantic Love*, further clarifies projection in relationships. "Human love sees another person as an individual and makes an individualized relationship to him or her. Romantic love sees the other person only as a role player in the drama." When a man projects romance on a woman or when a woman projects romance on a man, they never will be inwardly happy with the other person as they are.

Consciously interacting with others opens the way to developing friendships thus reducing the intense image projected on others. Friends enjoy, share, accept and affirm rather than find fault, judge and make unrealistic demands. Dr. Johnson writes, "In romantic love there is no friendship. Romance and friendship are utterly opposed energies, natural enemies with complete opposite motives."

Unconscious romantic "love" intensifies drama and toxicity. Conscious friendship is low drama and low maintenance. Romantic "love" is highly narcissistic, egocentric and high maintenance. Friendship love is thoughtful, understanding, patient, forgiving and reciprocal.

Here's a tip that may help you navigate the relationship world. If the other person uses the word "I" excessively and/or shows little or no self-observation, self-reflection or self-knowledge, see it as a red flag. If they are blamers rather than self-responsible, you may want to tread softly, go slow and/or excuse yourself.

Dr. Robert Sheldrake in his book *The Science Delusion* takes a non-materialistic view of life and of human relationships. He labels it morphic resonance. "The morphic field is within and around the system it organizes and is a vibratory pattern [energy] of activity that interacts with electromagnetic and quantum fields of the system."

He cites the identical twin research at the University of Minnesota established in 1989. The study revealed that identical twins separated at birth often have "patterns of activity, habits and health issues" influenced by morphic resonance. The Jim twins, both called James by their different adopted families, had similar life histories. Remarkably, they grew up in an only house on a block. The houses both had a tree in the backyard with a white bench around it. They both had passions for stock-car racing and making miniature picnic tables.

Reflect on your past and present relationships with friends, family and co-workers. Look at them through the lens of morphic resonance. What are you emanating and radiating mentally, emotionally and behaviorally? What are you registering from them by morphic resonance? What are they registering from you by morphic resonance?

Chapter 7: Summary

1. As a functioning energy being it's mandatory you withdraw projections. Projections are emotionally charged images in the mind that distort, fabricate and fantasize. When you project you are not in the moment, you are not registering the energy from the other person or energy from between you and the other person.
2. Romantic "love" is highly narcissistic, egocentric and high maintenance. Friendship love is thoughtful, understanding, patient, forgiving and reciprocal.

Chapter 8: Intuitive Energies

As you transition and process from a sense-based, unconscious person to an energy-oriented person, you will experience intuitive energies. Intuition is the conscious registration of knowing frequencies. In the digital-internet era we are often overwhelmed by information via words and images. This information is not direct knowing through experiential intuition. Often this form of information is not credible, accurate or useful. In other words, the map does not accurately show the territory. If you unconsciously follow it, you will experience frustrations, difficulties, problems, conflicts and misinformation.

Mental overload is a common problem for those living in an information saturated society. The information bombardment on the nervous system triggers a survival circuit breaker. Have you noticed yourself avoiding your email, text messages, social media, etc.? Your nervous system reaches an information limit and temporarily shuts down avoiding any additional input.

Intuition then becomes a necessity. You will feel-know when and what information is beneficial, useful, required and has priority. You will know without "thinking." The word thinking here means believing you need to give attention to every thought, word and image in order to find out what you need to know. Intuition skips this tedious and often exhausting process and homes in on the most required information.

On a visit to my friend Ronda's house I experienced intuitive energies. She asked, "Would you like something to drink?" I answered, "Yes." She responded, "I have tea or water." I paused for a half second for the intuition-feel. I replied, "Water." Ronda chose the store bottled ice tea.

I sipped the water. It was cold and refreshing especially on a hot California summer day. Ronda sipped the ice tea. She gasped, rushed to the kitchen sink and spit it out. She had not chosen intuitively. She commented that she wanted something with caffeine. This like thought in effect was a semantic blockage to the more benign intuitive information.

Ronda suggested we go for a foot massage. My initial feeling was I needed to be conscious in order to avoid picking up on and absorbing any negative energies. As a conscious, functioning energy being, you must pay attention to energies from people and places.

I failed to act on my intuition and went for the massage. The massage therapist was highly motivated and skilled. Regardless, I absorbed the energy of those who were on the massage table before me. I felt nauseated and had to excuse myself.

What's the difference between being psychic and being intuitive? When I was about 12 our family went on a vacation out West. One of our stops was at Teton National Park in Wyoming. We camped next to Jennie Lake at the base of the Grand Teton Mountain.

Early in the morning, just after sunrise we would sit by the lake's edge. When there was no wind, the surface of the lake was the proverbial smooth as glass. It reflected the 13,000-foot Grand Teton magnificently.

Being psychic is like the reflection on Jennie Lake of the Grand Teton. Being intuitive is seeing the Grand Teton directly. Once the wind came up Jennie Lake was no longer placid. Seeing the Grand Teton perfectly reflected was not possible. But it was still possible to see the Grand Teton directly by looking up at its magnificent heights.

Being "psychic" tends to be unconscious, automatic, intermittent, and not always reliable. At times, it can be clear and reflect beautifully and precisely like Jennie Lake. When automatic thinking and emotional reactivity increases, the psycho-logical winds blow making psychic impressions distorted, unreliable and false-to-fact.

Being "intuitive" is about consciously registering the frequencies directly without mental-emotional psychic static. As a conscious, functioning energy being, intuitive, direct perceptions organically arise in the moment. Focusing the concentrated mind on a person, place, thing, event or problem aligns your consciousness to receive intuitive energies. Holographic knowings flow into your awareness-field. You know what you need to know about a person, place, thing, event or problem.

Vitvan tells a story of a married couple he visited in Oakland, California. John was in business. He met a man who proposed a deal that potentially would make he and his wife rich. John called Mary from the office one day and told her he was bringing a possible new business partner home for dinner.

Mary cooked up one of her best recipes. The two businessmen talked and talked over a delicious home-cooked meal until the deal was struck. After the new partner left, Mary emphatically said, "John, do not go into business with that man." She repeated, "Do not go into business with that man." What did Mary know?

Well, within a week the deal fell through and John nearly lost everything. Dejected, demoralized and defeated John looked at his loving wife and asked, "Mary, how did you know? How did you know?" Mary replied, "I just knew."

Just as I finished writing about John and Mary my sister called. She moved back to Florida to live in her favorite community where previously she lived for thirty years. The day before she put a $150 deposit on a new place to live.

We all have a John and a Mary inside us. When she made the deposit on the modern, new apartment her John was doing the inner talking. "It has everything you want. There's a pool; it has two bedrooms; pets are allowed; it's affordable; it's a short drive to work." On the surface, it apparently was perfect. The logical John said, "Take it."

She called me after she woke up the next morning. Her inner Mary spoke, "John, don't move into that apartment." My sister realized she needed to live in a more private place with greater peace and quiet. Being a pre-school teacher demands a lot of energy. After work she's got to recharge.

The new, modern apartment had a main lobby she had to pass through in order to get to her apartment door. She realized the lobby had lots of people hanging out, a potential drain on her energy. Moreover, the apartment complex was a large one with hundreds of tenants. More possible distractions that could tug on her energy. Fortunately, she slept before making her final decision, allowing her intuitive Mary to get through to her consciousness as she woke up.

Summary: Chapter 8

1. Intuition is the conscious registration of knowing frequencies.
2. Your nervous system reaches an information limit and temporarily shuts down avoiding any additional input.
3. As a conscious functioning energy being, intuitive, direct perceptions organically arise in the moment.

Chapter 9: Creative Energies

Over the years I've heard many say I'm not creative. Usually they mean they can't draw, paint, sing, play a musical instrument, dance, write poetry, etc. This partly results from a misconception about what is creative energy. Creative energy flows from the invisible, inaudible frequencies to the visible, audible frequencies. When inspired or feeling a moment of profound sadness or joy, being playful or spontaneous, creative energy can spark and be expressed.

Creative energy is not always expressed artistically. Creative energy can be expressed in business, parenting, cooking, teaching – in almost any daily task. As a teacher I sometimes teach introductory poetry. Inevitably, there are students who say, "I can't write poetry. I can't think of anything." These automatic, unconscious statements are called semantic blockages. One of my mentors called them command phrases. They set up a barrier to the flow of creative energy.

When it comes to teaching poetry, I ask the students who say "I can't" to let go of the semantic blockage, command phrase. I ask them to write down the first word(s) that comes to mind requiring an act of self-observation. As usual I had a student respond by saying, "I can't think of anything." I gave him a nudge by asking him what he had for breakfast. "Pancakes," he replied. I told him to write that down and that he now had the first word of a poem.

He was skeptical giving me a look that said, "You have to be kidding me." I prompted him to write a second word. He said, "maple syrup." He wrote that down. I said, "You have your first line. Now put in a couple of rhymes." He caught the creative energy wave.

A few minutes later I returned to his desk. This is what he wrote.

Pancakes and maple syrup
I slurp and burp
Tastes so good

*I'd have it for breakfast
Every day if I could.*

    He went from I can't to a short, fun, humorous poem in matter of minutes. Rather than cling to I can't, be willing to see what happens. It helps to avoid labels like good and bad. Some of us have more of a natural talent in one artistic area over another. Expressing creative energy is not about good and bad; it's about experiencing a feeling of wholeness.

    Living in star consciousness, functioning as a star being, you become a conscious co-creator. When you tap into and express creative energy, you experience a connection with spiritual frequencies and an integrative, unifying feeling that dissipates the feeling of self-separateness. Creative energy is beyond time in the sense that time seems to stand still. Expressing creative energy for an hour in clock time may seem like only a few minutes have elapsed.

    Most children are naturally creative. Recall your childhood. You sang, danced, played a musical instrument, drew, painted, etc. without thinking or saying I can't. During the teen years the automatic thinking kicks in leading to sematic blockages and command phrases. This will dam up or restrict the flow of creative energy. There's a tendency to create less. The integrative, wholeness feelings that creative energy produces are experienced less. Warring thoughts, emotional conflicts, and seemingly insurmountable problems take center stage.

    A woman friend showed a lively interest in drawing and painting. In fact, she minored in art history while attending a large university. Her passion for the arts was so strong that she took a trip whose itinerary included the finest museums in the world.

    She looked, admired and appreciated the greatest artists the world has ever known. Deep in her heart she wished and hoped that she could create such beauty in color and form. Unfortunately, her wishes and hopes turned out to be nothing but faint inaudible inner whispers.

My woman friend suffered from three fairly common delusions about expressing creative energy: the delusion of inspiration, the delusion of perfection and the delusion of instant creation. She was blocked from tapping her creative energies by falsely believing that in order to draw or paint some inspirational idea had to magically enter her mind. Further, she believed that the inspiration would lift her into a mysterious world of creative ecstasy where instant creativity would flash on the paper or canvas. Finally, she falsely believed that the instant creative lightning bolt would produce a work of art equal to and maybe better than the masters.

Fortunately, my woman friend overcame her delusions around creativity. She met a musician-poet who saw her artistic potential. He encouraged her to draw. At first, she refused to try because of the delusions; but he persistently and with great patience continued to encourage her.

Finally, with reluctance, she bought a drawing pad, and some felt tip pens and began to draw. The color, the form, the designs, the beauty expressed amazed her. Creativity became a welcome and much needed joy in her life. A couple of years later she illustrated a book of poetry.

Annie Payson Call, who wrote for *Ladies Home Journal* for many years, described creative energy's effects.

"Art [creative energy] is immeasurably greater than we are. If we are free and quiet, the poem, the music, the picture will carry us, so that we shall be surprised at our own expression; and when we have finished, instead of being personally elated with conceited delight in what we have done, or exhausted with the superfluous effort used, we shall feel as if a strong wind blown through us and cleared us for better work in the future."

Summary: Chapter 9

1. When you tap into and express creative energy, you experience a connection with spiritual frequencies and an integrative, unifying feeling that dissipates the feeling of self-separateness.
2. Most children are naturally creative. Recall your childhood. You sang, danced, played a musical instrument, drew, painted, etc. without thinking or saying I can't.

Chapter 10: Transformative Energies

If you have conscientiously practiced expanding your consciousness by self-remembering, self-observation and self-reflection, you have noticed that at times you think, feel, speak, act, desire, etc. in ways that are self-destructive, activate negative energies and evoke abhorrent feelings. As you grow, evolve and advance toward star consciousness, you will become aware that you are capable of transforming lower frequency energies into higher frequency energies.

Some years ago I read Iris Chang's book, *The Rape of Nanking: The Forgotten Holocaust of WW II*. This book had a deep emotional impact on me. I was reflecting on what I read while driving. At a stop sign about a block from home, I noticed a man about 25 years old riding his bicycle down the cross street. I judged that I could easily stop, make a right turn and drive without coming close to interfering with the man's bike ride.

He felt different. He screamed, "You didn't stop buddy." With those words an intense mental-emotional storm whipped through my psyche. I thought, 'who the hell does he think he is. What a son-of-a-bitch.' Defensively, I thought, 'I wasn't anywhere close to him. I did stop. He doesn't know what he's saying.' Anger and defensiveness turned quickly to an inner rage.

I thought about turning back and confronting the bike rider. I visualized myself punching him out. Violent thoughts gave me a rush of adrenaline and a feeling of horror at my automatic thinking. Then it hit me like a punch in the stomach. I was resonating with the destructive energies. The young Japanese soldiers were conditioned to see the Chinese as vermin, justifying their diabolical death by ruthless murder and rape as perfectly okay, all in the name of the Emperor.

If I did not have a sense of horror by my violent reaction and begin to let it go, I could have gone to a diabolical place like the young Japanese soldier. Even though it was only a few seconds, I saw the bike rider as a less than human. If I hadn't been reading Chang's book and thinking intensely about the implications, I would not have seen the connection between my experience and the horrifically amplified violent expression experience by the Japanese soldier in 1937 Nanking.

I realized that childhood conditioning has a profound influence on the beliefs and actions of teens and young adults. I felt fortunate that the adult authorities in my younger life had stressed anger management, peaceful resolution and non-violence. These were strong values that I held deeply and cherished despite the fact that I did not always live up to them in an ideal way.

As a father of a teenage son at the time, I felt a much deeper sense of responsibility to instill non-violent values. I realized that a parent must do what they can to encourage and model peaceful resolution and sane compromise. It gets down to one adult and one child and a relationship where there's constructive mentoring. I realized that 1 + 1 + n leads to a global culture that deeply values peace in thoughts, feelings and actions in day-to-day life.

Many years ago I read another book, *Science and Sanity* by Polish engineer, Alfred Korzybski. He warned of the dangers of what he called the one-valued orientation. Reading *The Rape of Nanking* shed light on Korzybski's book. He predicted that a one-valued orientation like the one held by the Japanese toward the Chinese would lead to more world wars. He was prophetic.

The solution he proposed was the teaching of what he called the "consciousness of abstracting." In other words, when a person pays close attention to what he or she is seeing-experiencing in the moment, it creates what he referred to as the thalamic-cortical gap. The thalamus is the part of the nervous system that stores all the fight/flight instincts tapped into by the vicious Japanese in Nanking and by myself in anger toward the bike rider. He urged his readers to pause, count to ten, sleep on it, etc., allowing the nerve energy to move toward the cortex. In that way, the destructive thalamic energy could dissipate often leading to alternatives in thought, feeling, action and speech that were more thoughtful, compromising and compassionate. He labeled this the infinite-valued orientation.

Also, while reading *The Rape of Nanking* another author came to mind, the Swiss psychologist, Carl Jung. One of his major insights was the process of facing our shadow side. He made it clear that true freedom only comes when we face our dark past whether individual, family, community or country.

It's often monumentally difficult to face and transform the dark, shadow side of the personality. Memories of my darker moments bubbled up in my mind while reading Chang. I remembered the vicious fistfight with a classmate on the playground in third grade. I remembered the poundings I gave my younger brother when we were little. I remembered the brutal actions I took as a high school football player. One time I broke the leg of an opponent. I could write pages and pages about my shadow side.

Jung was right. By facing head on the dark side, lessons can be learned and there can be transformation. Until every textbook in Japan, until every textbook in every classroom everywhere shines light on the shadow of Nanking, the Japanese culture and the global culture will not have begun the deeper healing and learned the lessons of Nanking and how it applies to everyone's life.

As Chang writes on page 55, "Looking back upon millennia of history, it appears clear that no race or culture has a monopoly on wartime cruelty. The veneer of civilization seems to be exceedingly thin – one that can be easily stripped away, especially by the stresses of war."

In my book *Tuning to the Spiritual Frequencies*, Chapter 19, I provide eight ways to transform, transmute and regenerate your energies. (See how to order in the back of this book.) Isidore Friedman, my mentor for ten years, created the Alpha-Omega Circuit (see diagram on page 84) in order to transform your energies. Here is how you use it wisely and consciously.

Feel free to copy or draw the Alpha-Omega Circuit to a size that you can comfortably use. Place the Alpha-Omega

Circuit on a table or desk. Choose a space that's quiet and free of negative and/or distracting energies. Consider what would be wise to transform, reduce and/or eliminate from your life. It can be a bad habit, a negative thought or emotion, a pressure point of the past that holds you back from being fully conscious and functioning as an energy being.

Next, write down on a piece of paper what you want to let go of and place it over the two spiraling coils in the middle. Place your left thumb on Gamma, first finger of your of the left hand on Omikron and the middle finger of the left hand on Delta. Place the fingertips of the right hand on the squiggly line that ends in output.

Hold that position for about three minutes. Longer is not necessarily better. It's wiser to use the Alpha-Omega Circuit a little at a time, maybe once a week. After three minutes remove your hands and tear up the piece of paper and throw it away. Allow at least a half hour to rest and relax before resuming an active daily routine.

Pay attention to your energy level. Perhaps you require an hour or two of peace and quiet. Generally, your psyche needs time to adjust to the transformation of energy. Again, use the Alpha-Omega Circuit consciously and wisely along with the other ways given in *Tuning to the Spiritual Frequencies*.

Chapter 10: Summary

1. As you grow, evolve and advance toward star consciousness, you will become aware that you are capable of transforming lower frequency energies into higher frequency energies.
2. It's often monumentally difficult to face and transform the dark, shadow side of the personality.
3. By facing head on the dark side, lessons can be learned and there can be transformations.

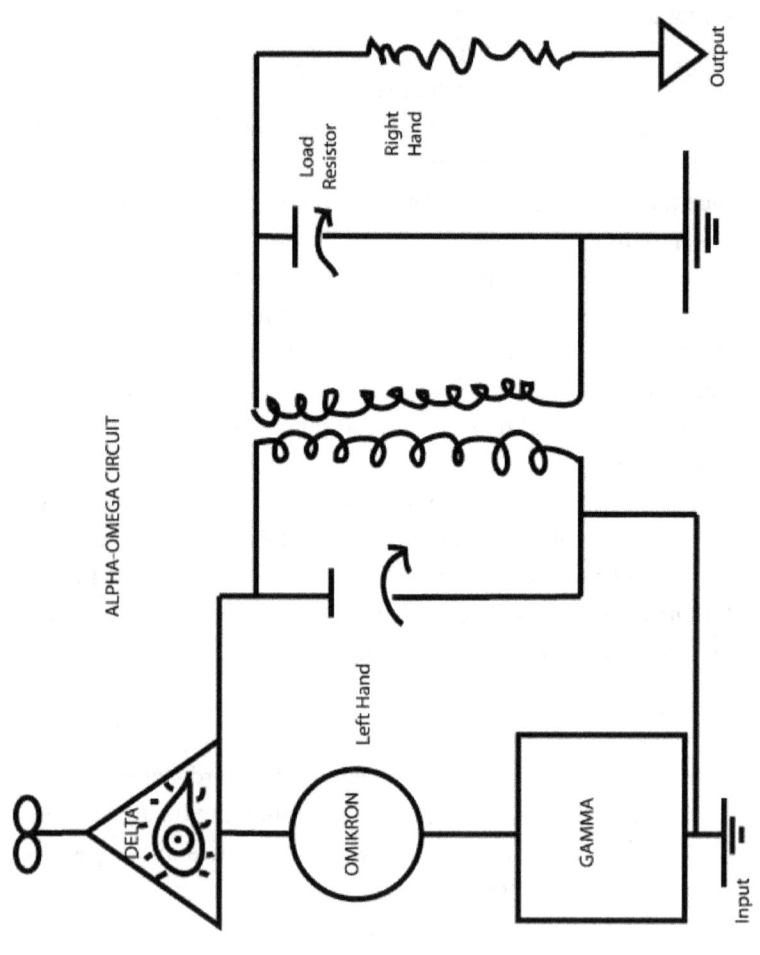

Alpha-Omega Circuit

Chapter 11: A Fully Functional Energy Being

If you are still reading this small book, hopefully much of what you have read has connected with your consciousness as meaningful, beneficial and practical. Perhaps you have read straight through to this point. Or, maybe you have read bits and pieces overtime. Regardless, I have attempted to show a star path to expanding your consciousness and developing as a fully functional energy being.

Some of you like myself grew up immersed in materialistic consumerism. The unsane pursuit of more and more "things" and the belief that "success" is measured by the house, the car, the gadgets, the physical appearance, the jewelry, the social ranking from super rich to super poor eventually leads to an existential dead end and spiritual bankruptcy. Moreover, blindly accepting and identifying with comatose unconsciousness seemed to be the way to go, the order of the day. Why in the world expand your consciousness and transform from a "thing" based, "physical" only person to a functional energy being who reflects star consciousness?

Over more than a half century on the expanding consciousness path I have met those who in many ways are already energy beings but they don't know it. Even worse and sadly they have never received any training on how to direct, manage and transform their energies. This small book is dedicated to you. The urgency of this information, if applied and continuously practiced, potentially will restore equilibrium in your consciousness on a day to day basis.

Remember from second to second, morning, noon and night - even while you sleep - you are a configuration of energy units (photons) in a dynamic energy world. You must practice this admonition until you register-feel the energies emanating subtly from people, places and "things". Then you will let go more and more your identification with materialism and experience joy, happiness, purpose, understanding, wisdom, compassion, etc. – the spiritual frequencies.

You might think or ask, "How long with it take?" I would suggest you hold off asking this question and devote a minimum of two years to directing, managing and transforming your energies more consciously. Test it. See what happens. If you experience more physical repose, emotional calm and peace of mind, then keep going. Perhaps you will eventually transition and identify with star consciousness: the skill and wisdom to direct, manage and transform energy.

How does a fully functioning energy being behave, act, live?
Values being conscious
Diligently practices being conscious
Identifies with energy
Detaches from things
Know they are more than a physical body
Does not blame or alibi
Conscious of motivating forces, frequencies and energies
Feels compassion for others
Consciously assists others
Respects the free will of others
Does not control others
Practices rhythmic alternation
Persistently practices the purificatio
Avoids ego inflation
Feels and shares conscious love
Consciously co-creates
Uses measured speech
Knows how and when to go into neutral
Cultivates determination
Manages and transforms energy rapports
Practices whole living
Practices gratitude
Practices cooperation
Directs, Manages, Transforms Energy

"Objective" science is beginning to embrace "subjective" science. This removes an old, encrusted energy blockage allowing each to take the hero/heroine journey to star consciousness, light, love, wisdom, understanding, happiness and becoming a conscious co-creator.

Dr. Rupert Sheldrake summed it up in the article *Setting Science Free from Materialism*.

Contemporary science is based on the claim that all reality is material or physical. There is no reality but material reality. Consciousness is a by-product of the physical activity of the brain. Matter is unconscious. Evolution is purposeless. This view is now undergoing a credibility crunch. The biggest problem of all materialism is the existence of consciousness. Panpsychism provides a way forward. So does the recognition that minds are not confined to brains.

In the early 2000s my son, Dane, attended Pepperdine University. He took a film class with Tom Shadyac, director of *Liar Liar, Ace Ventura* and *Bruce Almighty*. By any measure, Shadyac was one of the most "successful" Hollywood directors at that time.

I visited Dane at Pepperdine and he arranged for me to attend the film class. It was fun, energizing and humorous. Dane introduced me to Tom. He insisted everyone call him Tom. Tom was gracious and genuinely friendly.

After class, Dane told me Tom rode his bike to work, to the store, to Pepperdine – most everywhere. Additionally, he donated his time as a teacher at Pepperdine. I wondered what had happened to him that changed his life from being a rich Hollywood tycoon to a less materialistic, more purposeful community service guy.

The next day Dane and I went to the local Malibu grocery store to shop for dinner. As we were about to enter the store, Tom, riding his racing bike, pulls up to the entrance. He remembers me, and he calls Dane by name. Impressive. I asked him what he was working on? He told us he was creating his first documentary about a life changing experience. It wasn't the time or place to go into detail about the project. We parted ways and did our grocery shopping.

A few months later Dane called letting me know Tom's documentary, *I Am*, was released. He told me it was a must see and that it resonated with my own experiences, writing and teaching. *I Am* chronicles Tom's life-threatening mountain bike accident. He suffered a broken hand and a life altering concussion, post-concussion syndrome (PCS). He was essentially helpless. He was continuously disoriented, experienced perpetual ringing in the ears and agonized over hypersensitivity to lights and sounds. After months of agony, he welcomed death.

He asked himself a profound question – "What is wrong with the world and what can we do about it?" As he investigated by interviewing the greatest minds of the time, he came to realize the world had a "ever growing addiction to materialism."

This discovery prompted him to make some fundamental life changes. He sold his sprawling multimillion dollar Pasadena estate. He moved into a more modest upscale trailer park in North Malibu. He devoted his time, energy and money to writing, producing and directing *I Am*. He accepted his call to adventure and took the hero journey from near death to finding a purposeful life. Essentially, he evolved into a conscious functioning energy being.

As of this writing, 2018, Tom teaches film at the University of Memphis and supports non-profits through his foundation. He is much happier. He even produced a documentary titled *Happy*.

Chapter 11: Summary

1. Remember from second to second, morning, noon and night – even while you sleep – you are a configuration of energy units (photons) in a dynamic energy world.

You must practice this admonition until you register-feel the energies emanating subtly from people, places and "things."
2. You might think or ask, "How long will it take?" I would suggest you hold off asking this question and devote a minimum of two years to directing, managing and transforming your energies more consciously.
3. Test it. See what happens. If you experience more physical repose, emotional calm and peace of mind, then keep going.
4. Objective science is beginning to embrace subjective science. This removes and old, encrusted energy blockage allowing each to take the hero/heroine journey to star consciousness, light, love, wisdom, understanding, happiness and becoming a conscious co-creator.

Chapter 12: Aligning With Star Consciousness

Go soft, go slow, go cool, go far
Structure your Being as a Rising Star
Break self-imposed chain of illusioned speech
That the One Infinity may your freedom teach.

Gird your loins for the battle grim
That race-ignorance darkness in you may trim
The word-concept prison in which you lie
And struggle and complain and innerly die.

Be conscious, and seek the pulsing Light
To lift you from emotion's boiling point
Calm your mind, your heart, and train your hand
That on Perception's moment you eventually stand.

Break the darkness of unconscious speech
That lying words of the profiteer's screech
Strengthen your hear and light your mind
From the race-mind and animals your Being unbind.

Your Attention, Choice, Decision make
From unconscious emotion to forever break,
And strong and cool in the Shining Star
With swords of trained mind, ignorance to bar.

From Songs of the Starlords by Isidore Friedman

As more and more of us are finding out and deeply knowing, money alone does not buy happiness. By valuing and practicing being conscious – mindful, aware, observing, perceiving, seeing, etc. – we align and resonate our energies with a greater participation in our life path and purpose, which is more valuable than things, than money, than success, than fame.

How can you know this is true? Try it. Give it a month.

See what happens. Prove it or disprove it. Practice being conscious all day every day for a month. Notice how you feel. Notice the empowerment and experience of accelerated energy. Being more conscious, even for a minute or two, resonates with frequencies more harmonious, rhythmic and balanced. Your firsthand experience provides an incentive to practice being more and more conscious. When you forget being conscious, practice again and again. Eventually, it will be a wonderful life enriching habit.

What differentiates humans from animals is the function of being conscious. Functionally, being conscious requires a choice to self-remember, self-observe and self-reflect – to be continuously mindful and alert. Doing this necessitates steady effort and self-monitoring.

We spend most of our time-energy automatically doing, thinking, feeling, sleeping, eating, talking, desiring, etc. Naturally, habitual actions are useful. Once we learn something, we can do it without thinking. Being conscious, however, brings our attention into the moment and activates and energizes the mind-body-consciousness force-field, aligning us with the spiritual frequencies, star consciousness.

Materialistic, sense-based societies, nations, cultures do not value and encourage being conscious. This mindless and unconscious behavior detunes us from our core star consciousness and robs us of the heightened experience of being more fully alive. Don't believe, test. Make it a daily practice to be more conscious. Stick with it. At first, the benefits may not be apparent. But with continuous practice you will experience alignment and resonance with star consciousness.

Consciousness is axiomatic. It needs no proof. Vitvan words it this way: "But when we say there is a power to be conscious, it cannot be challenged; because let somebody challenge it and you can turn right around and say, with what power do you challenge? With what power do you doubt? etc.

Once you are a fully functioning energy being you will gradually, and at times not so gradually, align and resonate with star consciousness. You will consciously identify with the power to be conscious. Alvin Boyd Kuhn in his book *The Lost Light* words it in more symbolic terms: "Cutoff from our full solar light [star consciousness] in the darkness of incarnation [unconscious sense-based], we still have the divine light [star consciousness] by reflection upon our physical lives. The moonlight [energy being consciousness] is not that true light, but it bears witness to that light."

Vitvan expresses it differently in his book *Natural Order Process*. "Every field must therefore be described as a field of Light in the Light. The higher the level respecting the development of consciousness, the brighter the Light. We know from definite experience that these fields are brighter than the noonday sun and constitute the Light of all levels of the real world." In the beginning of this book I provided a referent for star consciousness, the skill and wisdom to direct, manage and transform energy. To that I now add the skill and wisdom to direct, manage and transform lightergy.

Consciousness is axiomatic. It is experienced in the silence on the non-verbal level. We may not be able to say fundamentally what consciousness is. Nevertheless, we can observe and experience how it functions. Consciousness can expand and contract. Consciousness can be conscious of itself. Consciousness increases most in the moment, the Eternal Now. Consciousness is creative, playful and loving. Choosing and practicing being conscious improves sensory awareness, amplifies understanding, resonates with happiness, joy, compassion and purpose. Star consciousness is free. Choose to be conscious. Be the best you can be – a conscious star.

> *Every man has a little spark of the sun in his bosom ... a spark of the original light is supposed to remain deep down in the interior of every atom.*
>
> Hargrave Jennings, Rosicrucian, 1872

And this I know: whether the one True Light
Kindle to Love, or Wrath consume me quite,
One glimpse of It within the tavern caught
Better than in the temple lost outright.

From *Rubaiyat of Omar Khayyam*

The esotericist understands that true self-knowledge can be attained only through self-development in the highest possible sense of the term, a development which begins with introspection and the awakening of creative and regenerative forces which now slumber in man's inner protoplasmic nature, like the vivific potency in the ovum, and which when roused into activity transforms him ultimately into a divine being bodied in a deathless ethereal form of ineffable beauty.

James M. Pryse, *The Apokalypse Unsealed*

One is able to see a beatific glow radiating above and around all objects and things. It appears like a shimmering, silvery aura and turns the mundane world into a fairyland.

Vitvan

Chapter 12: Summary

1. By valuing and practicing being conscious – mindful, aware, observing, perceiving, seeing, etc. – you align and resonate your energies with a greater participation in your life path and purpose, which is more valuable that things, than money, than success, than fame.
2. Being more conscious, even for a minute or two, resonates with frequencies more harmonious, rhythmic and balanced.

3. Functionally, being conscious requires a choice to self-remember, self-observe and self-reflect – to be continually mindful and alert. Doing this necessitates steady effort and self-monitoring.
4. Being conscious, however, brings our attention into the moment and activates and energizes the mind-body-consciousness force-field, aligning us with spiritual frequencies, star consciousness.
5. Once you are a fully functioning energy being you will gradually, and at times not so gradually, align and resonate with star consciousness. You will consciously identify with the power to be conscious.
6. Consciousness can expand and contract. Consciousness can be conscious of itself. Consciousness increases most in the moment, the Eternal Now. Consciousness is creative, playful and loving. Choosing and practicing being conscious improves sensory awareness, amplifies understanding, resonates with happiness, joy, compassion and purpose.

Epilog

From the NASA Lunar Science Institute:
Before you judge others or claim any absolute truth, consider that…you can see less than 1% of the electromagnetic spectrum and hear less than 1% of the acoustic spectrum. As you read this, you are traveling at 220 kilometers per second across the galaxy. 90% of the cells in your body carry their own microbial DNA and are not "you". The atoms in your body are 99.9999999999999999% empty space and none of them are the ones you were born with, but they all originated in the belly of a star. Human beings have 46 chromosomes, 2 less than the common potato. The existence of the rainbow depends on the conical photoreceptors in your eyes; to animals without cones, the rainbow does not exist. So you don't just look at a rainbow, you create it. This is pretty amazing, especially considering that all the beautiful colors you see represent less than 1% of the electromagnetic spectrum.

Appendix

Origin of the word Star:

Osiris, Sir, Czar, Lazarus, Caesar, Kaiser, Pastor, Master, Minister, Magistrate are all variations of the word star. One who consciously practices directing, managing and transforming their life energy is a true star. As a Star their life path is illumined as often are the paths of those around them. One who functions in Star Consciousness is an authority. Thor is another variation on the word Star.

Vitvan's Introduction to Meditation – *from Self-Mastery Through Meditation*:

Do you know that there must be a circuit or there is nothing? Do you know that if the submicroscopic vortices of negative energy that we label electrons, did not describe a circuit then there would be no atom, and, therefore, no molecules, no cellular structure, no 'thing'? I want to show you that what we call the universe rests upon structure-function circuits-energy circuits.

And how is energy described? Energy is described as units of light. Go back to the first chapter of the Book of Genesis: "Let there be light" which can be paraphrased to read "Let there be units of light, photons, the first emergence." But those units of light, electrons, etc., describe a circuit. All that we are conscious of being, all that we are conscious of, is nothing except the peripheries of circuits. "God is all in all" is just another way of saying it. But it is the circuit, in factor number two, which I would now call to your attention.

It is the negative wave that first leaps to the positive pole which completes the circuit.

Go to meditation. In its process, one must direct all of his "first fruits"—that is, his forces or energies—to the Power with which he is conscious. What is the "first fruit" anyone is conscious of? It is the energy which is used in generation: it is this energy which is offered. That is what I call meditation. And anything short of that I will not call meditation. If, in oneself, he wants to complete the circuit, he must first make this offering. I do not want to hold on to my objective self-conscious state and expect something to come to me. I have to give myself first.

The seed is cast into the earth. Unless it dies it produces no fruit. "He who gives up his life for my sake shall find it." The whole point hinges on the surrender, giving up, offering in genuineness, in sincerity—almost in desperation—offering it all. The conscious direction of generative energy and surrender of it is the positive attitude, as it requires sustained effort and will and is, therefore, not a supine relaxation. In this directive way we say: Release, renounce, let go. Offer your force, offer your energy, give it up, surrender, let the energies or forces leap to the positive pole. And... bang! The circuit is completed, the fire descends—then, Light.

I am trying to describe to you my idea of meditation. It is not sitting supinely waiting for something to come to you; it is you that has to give. I am reversing the former idea. Let us get down to the little steps, where even a child could not err.

If you are not conscious of any force in any center, or if you are not conscious of having centers in your psychic nature or of any frequency in any center, then focus your thought at the crown of your head. As you center your thought, close your eyes and look up there and hold your thought steadily, in and up, at the crown. Then imagine, will, as you hold your thought steadily, that all of your forces, energies, etc., are flowing to that point. Imagine, will, and direct all of your energies to that point with the idea that you are rendering an offering to that deeper or greater Power—the heart, the core, the root of your being, the Power with which you think, feel and act. Offer it; hold your attention steadily; do not let it go away. If it goes away, pull it back until it stays there.

I am often asked, "How long shall I do it?" Do it until it stays there of itself. I have found some who practice it a few weeks and it stays there: "they enter the Father's house and go out therefrom no more." I have had others who have worked for years, spasmodically, with little or no results. Keep on offering. Remember, your offering must be accepted before the fire descends. Be patient and never become weary in well-doing, because you will "reap if you faint not." It is those who faint by the wayside who never succeed.

Hold the attention steady. Breathe air into the lungs while your attention is held steady at the crown, and you will vitalize yourself with more energy. In every way you can devise, imagine, will, and direct all your force there at the top of the head.

Do you see that this is positive? You are working to offer the negative force to the positive center.

I cannot put it in plainer words. But I am going to ask you, what are you going to do about it? I have done this for so many years I have forgotten how not to do it. Now that I have gotten on to the trick, I focus, will, breathe, think my energies are flowing there. I drive a tractor, help the carpenters, hoe corn in the garden, and I never relax from that effort: I keep focused while I am doing anything else. This is what I call "prayer without ceasing." I am in a constant state of prayer. I don't have to go and sit down, because I have practiced it for so long that I can keep on practicing no matter what I am doing. And this is what I call meditation. I am busy and active in a constant state of meditation.

I want to emphasize the importance of cultivating this attitude, for you must not be caught on a lower level, as the maelstrom increases in the world around you. You must fortify yourself as rapidly as possible. Reach this "Secret Place of the Most High."

Great peace, sense of security, great happiness and joy result through this meditation. It is so wonderful that it remains forever on the unspeakable level. What could one say to describe its beauty? Nothing. But we live in its radiance, we live in its joy song, we live in its beauty to such an extent that if we lower our focus for just a little bit, we quickly return, because we have become conditioned to its Ananda, to its beauty, its ecstasy.

Vitvan School of the Natural Order (Library of Books & Audio)
P.O. Box 150, Baker, Nevada 89311
Email: sno@sno.org
Website: http://www.sno.org

Isidore Friedman: Books and Notebooks on Organics available on Patreon - Greg Nielsen: Writing, Video & Audio available on Patreon Published Books available on Amazon.com Author Page: https://www.amazon.com/Greg-Nielsen/e/B001JCG5IY/ref=ntt_dp_epwbk_0

Conscious Books
316 California Avenue, Ste. 210
Reno, Nevada 89509

Email: spiritualfrequenciesonline@gmail.com

Website: http://spiritualfrequencies.weebly.com/

Facebook: https://www.facebook.com/Spiritual-Frequencies-Online-Academy-1436072066656123/?ref=bookmarks

Instagram: spiritualfrequenciesacademy

Twitter: @FrequenciesDrG

YouTube Channel: https://www.youtube.com/channel/UCA8Rwm6Xl-4C8D131dqAkeIw?

Patreon.com: Where you can become a patron and financially support Spiritual Frequencies Online Academy for a modest monthly subscription. Patreon.com/spiritualfrequencies

Venmo: contribute directly to Conscious Books credit union account: @Greg-Nielsen-9

www.ingramcontent.com/pod-product-compliance
Lightning Source LLC
Chambersburg PA
CBHW071726040426
42446CB00011B/2241